The USSR's Emerging Multiparty System

THE WASHINGTON PAPERS

. . . intended to meet the need for an authoritative, yet prompt, public appraisal of the major developments in world affairs.

President, CSIS: David M. Abshire

Series Editor: Walter Laqueur

Director of Publications: Nancy B. Eddy

Managing Editor: Donna R. Spitler

MANUSCRIPT SUBMISSION

The Washington Papers and Praeger Publishers welcome inquiries concerning manuscript submissions. Please include with your inquiry a curriculum vitae, synopsis, table of contents, and estimated manuscript length. Manuscripts must be between 120–200 double-spaced typed pages. All submissions will be peer reviewed. Submissions to *The Washington Papers* should be sent to *The Washington Papers*; The Center for Strategic and International Studies; 1800 K Street NW; Suite 400; Washington, DC 20006. Book proposals should be sent to Praeger Publishers; One Madison Avenue; New York NY 10010.

The Washington Papers/148

The USSR's Emerging Multiparty System

Vera Tolz

Foreword by S. Frederick Starr

Published with The Center for
Strategic and International Studies
Washington, D.C.

PRAEGER

New York
Westport, Connecticut
London

Library of Congress Cataloging-in-Publication Data

Tolz, Vera.
    The USSR's emerging multiparty system / Vera Tolz.
        p.   cm. – (The Washington papers, ISSN 0278-937X ; 148)
    Includes index.
        ISBN 0-275-93838-7 (alk. paper). – ISBN 0-275-93839-5 (pbk. :
    alk. paper)
        1. Political parties – Soviet Union – History.   2. Soviet
    Union – Politics and government – 1985-   3. Perestroïka.   I. Title.
    II. Series.
    JN6598.A1T65   1990
    324.247′009 – dc20   90-45046

The *Washington Papers* are written under the auspices of The Center
for Strategic and International Studies (CSIS) and published
with CSIS by Praeger Publishers. The views expressed in these papers
are those of the authors and not necessarily those of the Center.

British Library Cataloguing-in-Publication data is available.

Library of Congress Catalog Card Number: 90-45046
ISBN: 0-275-93838-7 (cloth)
        0-275-93839-5 (paper)

First published in 1990

Praeger Publishers, One Madison Avenue, New York, NY 10010
An imprint of Greenwood Publishing Group, Inc.

Printed in the United States of America

∞

The paper used in this book complies with the Permanent
Paper Standard issued by the National Information Standards
Organization (Z39.48-1984).

10 9 8 7 6 5 4 3 2 1

91-1143

Contents

Foreword

Nothing is more central to the democratization of the USSR than the abolition of the Communist Party's monopoly of power and the establishment of alternative parties protected by law. This process, which is both the means and end of true reform, largely occurred between 1987 and 1990, the period covered by Vera Tolz's monograph. It is amply evident these years constitute a watershed in Russian history, comparable in importance to 1917–1920, 1905–1907, and 1861–1864.

What fundamental forces brought about this epochal change? Many observers have traced it to the government's decision in the spring of 1988 to encourage the establishment of "popular fronts" to back its reform program. Tolz makes clear that this was Gorbachev's purpose in allowing Tatiana Zaslavskaya, Boris Kurashvili, and others to put out the call to set up such groups. But it was a serious miscalculation. Within months large parts of the public had moved well ahead of the government and were demanding reforms far more radical than those advocated by Gorbachev and the Communist Party.

This should not have been a surprise. Soviet public opinion, previously atomized and inchoate, was now crystalizing in new voluntary associations and clubs. Even before the 1988 decision, such informal groups were successfully bringing their influence to bear on governmental decisions and the allocation of resources. In other words, they were already creating new politics "from below." Their appearance represents the largest outpouring of public initiative in Russia since the early twentieth century.

Of particular importance in Tolz's monograph is her description of the Communist Party's efforts to retard and control this public outpouring. It is revealing that even the reform-minded journals *Ogonek* and *Moscow News* suppressed much vital information on the important Moscow conclave of voluntary associations held in August 1987. On something as important as unauthorized politics, there were limits to *glasnost*. The party's efforts to suppress the first fully proclaimed alternative party, the Democratic Union, and its patronage of both the "Interfront" groups in the Baltic republics and the United Front of Workers in Russia attest to the old regime's active resistance to what in retrospect may seem to have been an inevitable development.

The process of establishing alternative parties is not yet complete at this writing. More than three dozen new political parties existed in the USSR by 1990, but none enjoy the full protection of law. The thousands of local voluntary groups that sustain these parties still lack a clear legal existence, and the legislation that would address this need remains locked up in bureaucratic debate. The sheer complexity of the task of creating political pluralism attests to the thoroughness with which the Marxist-Leninist regime was instituted between 1917 and 1985.

In spite of the difficulties and negative pressures it describes, the overall picture presented by Tolz's monograph is of a civil society in the making. Unless the currents described herein are abruptly checked by some force not yet visible on the Soviet political horizon, they will lead not to some halfway house between totalitarianism and democracy—that is, to Gorbachev's old notion of pluralism within the Communist Party or Fedor Burlatsky's idea of a qualified "civil socialist society"—but to a democratic and relatively open system based on law rather than force and fully compatible with those now prevailing from the Atlantic Ocean to Anatolia and from Lapland to Sicily.

S. Frederick Starr
President, Oberlin College

September 1990

About the Author

Vera Tolz is a senior research analyst in the Radio Liberty Research Department. In 1981 she graduated from Leningrad University, where she studied classical philology and Russian literature. She is currently a Ph.D. candidate at the Centre for Russian and East European Studies at the University of Birmingham (England). A regular contributor to the *Report on the USSR* of Radio Liberty and other journals of Soviet studies, Tolz compiled *The USSR in 1989: A Record of Events* (1990).

Acknowledgments

I thank my colleagues in the Radio Liberty Research Department, especially Ann Sheehy, Elizabeth Teague, and Julia Wishnevsky, for sharing with me their knowledge and experience. I also thank Elizabeth Hayes for her proofreading of the manuscript.

Invaluable research help was provided by the Radio Liberty Samizdat Department, which keeps the West's largest collection of unofficial journals and programs of independent sociopolitical movements in the Soviet Union.

Summary

The Soviet media claim that informal groups first appeared in the early 1960s. In fact, throughout the history of the USSR, groups of like-minded people have gathered, without official permission, to discuss issues of common interest. They had their predecessors in prerevolutionary voluntary associations and political parties. During the 1960s, to which the Soviet press refers as the birth date of the first unofficial organizations, it simply became easier and less dangerous than in the previous period of Stalin's rule to engage in activities outside government control. Indeed, since the de-Stalinization campaign in the 1950s, Soviet society has been slowly asserting its independence, at least in areas nominally nonpolitical. Nevertheless, until Gorbachev's drive for liberalization achieved some momentum, the creation of unsanctioned groups often continued to provoke persecution of their members.

From the time that voluntary associations of Soviet people were permitted to emerge from the underground and openly participate in official public life (1987), their role in the political and social life of the country has been rapidly expanding. By 1989, new sociopolitical groups, especially in the Baltic republics and Transcaucasia, started to pose not only a challenge but also a threat to the power of the Communist Party of the Soviet Union (CPSU). In 1990, primarily because of pressure from these unofficial movements, the CPSU was forced to relinquish its constitutionally guaranteed monoploy on power. In other words, a multiparty system had de facto emerged in the USSR by the end of the period under observation in this book.

The emergence of a multiparty system in the Soviet Union, with various political groups pursuing different—and at times opposing—goals, is coinciding with a period during which the central authorities are being inconsistent in implementing democratic reforms, and a legal basis for democratic changes already de facto achieved still does not exist. Representatives of new movements are often politically inexperienced, and the CPSU is facing a serious crisis, which makes the political situation in the Soviet Union highly unpredictable and highlights the difficulties that the country faces in moving toward a more democratic system.

The USSR's Emerging Multiparty System

1

Introduction

The political landscape in the Soviet Union, which had long been the preserve of a sole and seemingly perennial sovereign party, has been teeming with new undergrowth during the past three years. Reborn, restructured, and freshly formed parties, groups, and movements have appeared and developed quickly; some of them have already stood the test of multicandidate elections. These organizations embrace a broad cross section of the Soviet population, including representatives of virtually every age range and professional group. Political views of their members and supporters also vary widely, ranging from the "left" (in Soviet terminology, those who advocate Western-style parliamentary democracy and a market economy) to the "right" (monarchists and those who denounce private property and advocate preserving the integrity of the Soviet empire).

This volume traces the history in the Soviet Union of this new and unaccustomed political pluralism, which began in 1986 when unsanctioned organizations (called informal groups or *neformal'nye gruppy* in the Soviet press) tentatively emerged from the underground and cautiously attempted to participate in public life. The activization of extant unofficial groups and the formation of new ones are the result of Soviet leader Mikhail Gorbachev's reformist policies, which have included an appeal to the Soviet people to participate more actively in public life. Another factor, and one that seems almost equally important, has been the gradual but steady political maturation of Soviet society, which has occurred during the past several decades and which might be viewed as a burgeoning revolution from below.

In launching *perestroika*, the Soviet leadership clearly acknowledged the need to stimulate independent activities among Soviet citizens. Statements by Soviet leaders revealed an awareness of a connection between economic problems and the suppression of public initiative. One of the architects of Gorbachev's reforms, Politburo member Aleksandr Yakovlev, adequately summed up the pre-*perestroika* situation, saying that "the administrative command system created under Stalin in the 1930s and 1940s allowed the State to swallow up civil society. The result led to economic stagnation."[1]

Initially, however, the authorities hoped to keep unsanctioned activities under strict control. They intended to stimulate activities in the social sphere while suppressing those in the political sphere. Clearly, the architects of *perestroika* had in mind only a limited relaxation of the state's power vis-à-vis the society at large. Describing what he called "a civil socialist society," political commentator Fedor Burlatsky defined the division of responsibility between the state and society in the following way:

> The state can provide for domestic order and national security. It can protect those below the poverty line and the small nationalities. It can ensure basic human rights, save society from excessive differentiation in income, and provide for a basic standard of living. But the state cannot directly control the economy, the development of culture, or public and private morality. These are the responsibility of a civil society.[2]

This definition does not include permission for independent political activities by unofficial groups. Events have not, however, unfolded as the leadership evidently envisaged that they would. By 1989, the role of unofficial organizations had expanded to such an extent that their activities began to pose a challenge to the Communist Party. This challenge was well demonstrated for the first time during the elections to the USSR Congress of People's Deputies in the spring of 1989. Then the congress itself voted early in 1990 to abolish the provision of the Soviet Constitution guaranteeing the CPSU's monopoly on power.

This volume also examines the response of the authorities to the challenge represented by unofficial groups and concludes that efforts to exercise control over those groups have largely failed. In 1988, the authorities believed that the organization of popular fronts would control the informal movement and neutralize the most radical groups. The ruling elite, however, underestimated the extent to which the popular fronts would themselves begin to advance far-reaching proposals rather than draw people away from radical informal associations. It seems that in 1989 the authorities dropped the ambitious task of elaborating a general policy to regulate informal groups. They did not, however, cease to attempt to influence individual unofficial organizations—mainly by infiltrating them.

The nature of this response and other problems facing unofficial organizations, including the lack of a tradition of political initiative outside the CPSU, are cogent reminders that the existence of a plurality of parties does not mean that the Soviet Union has already been transformed into a democratic society. This transformation probably will face difficulties and will take time.

Finally, it must be remembered that because there are thousands of sociopolitical movements in the USSR today, not all of them can be described in this volume. Attention has thus been given only to those that are the most politically mature and influential. These include various popular

fronts in the Soviet republics as well as major political organizations established in Moscow in 1989 and 1990. The
second largest city of the Soviet Union, Leningrad, also
merits special attention because it was there that one of the
major unofficial conservative antireform organizations—
the United Front of Workers—was born.

Predecessors of Contemporary
Unofficial Movements

When discussing groups and movements whose establishment is not officially sanctioned, the Soviet media usually
use the term "informal" (*neformal 'nyi*). Some of these organizations are later officially registered and, strictly
speaking, are no longer informal or unofficial. But, as will
be demonstrated later, the authorities have often continued
to treat these groups as though they have no legal basis.

The Soviet media claim that informal groups first appeared in the early 1960s.[3] In fact, throughout the history
of the USSR, groups of like-minded peers have gathered,
without official permission, to discuss issues of common
interest. They also had predecessors in prerevolutionary
voluntary associations that began to emerge as a result of
the reforms of the 1860s. In 1917 there were more than 300
voluntary scientific societies alone.[4]

Moreover, the Manifesto of October 17, 1905, and the
subsequently adopted Constitution of April 23, 1906, legalized the establishment in Russia of political parties that did
not seek to initiate a revolutionary coup. The elections to
the first and second State Dumas (in March 1906 and in
January 1907) were marked by the victory of democratic
and leftist candidates, as were the elections to the Congress
of People's Deputies of the USSR in the spring of 1989.

The czarist regime treated the first and the second
Dumas much more harshly than the current Soviet leader-
ship has thus far treated the Soviet parliament, but the
Duma deputies were more radical in their proposals and

much less willing to compromise with those in power than the deputies of today's Soviet parliament have been. After the revolution in February 1917, the Provisional Government announced the establishment of full civil liberties, including freedom for independent political activities.

The October Revolution and the period of War Communism caused some voluntary societies to be abolished. Soon after the October Revolution, the Bolsheviks banned any political opposition in the country. Some nonpolitical voluntary associations remained, however, and new ones continued to appear throughout the 1920s. Moreover, until the end of the 1920s, a number of unofficial groups existed whose members were engaged in studying historical, cultural, and scientific questions without much interference from the authorities in their activities.[5] The so-called regional studies (*kraevedenie*) movement, for example, which existed until the end of the 1920s, was relatively informal. In 1927, according to the journal of the Section of the Scientific Workers, *Nauchnyi rabotnik*, many of the 2,000 organizations for regional studies existed without official registration.[6]

At the end of the 1920s and the beginning of the 1930s, voluntary associations were abolished and many of their members were arrested. Commenting about the crackdown on voluntary scientific organizations in 1930, the Soviet press wrote that "the October revolution should finally penetrate into those corners that have been carefully closed from it, for instance, into voluntary scientific societies, which managed to survive in their archaic immunity."[7]

Even in the worst period of Stalin's rule, however, according to recollections of witnesses, some young people organized groups to discuss issues of common interest—although these gatherings often ended in the arrest of the groups' participants.[8] During the 1960s, which the Soviet press considers the birth date of the first informal groups, it simply became easier and less dangerous to conduct activities outside government control than it had been under Stalin.

Indeed, since the de-Stalinization campaign in the

1950s, Soviet society has been slowly asserting its independence, at least in the nominally nonpolitical areas. As the British journalist Martin Walker noted, "The country went through a social revolution while Brezhnev slept." During the past three decades, the USSR as a whole has become more urban, better educated, and more open. Despite official disapproval, Soviet youth has embraced Western pop culture, while scholars and scientists have sought contacts with their colleagues in the West. The post-Stalin years have witnessed a tremendous resurgence of independent culture, the appearance of political *samizdat* writings, and the establishment of vocal human rights movements. Voices in the non-Russian republics have persistently clamored for the preservation of the national language and heritage.

In the past two decades, those advocating the sovereignty of the republics or even their independence from the Soviet Union have begun to be heard. These human rights and nationalist movements of the 1960s and the 1970s are prototypes of today's sociopolitical movements. Moreover, some of these earlier movements currently continue their activities. Between the 1960s and the beginning of the 1980s, behind the staid and seemingly immutable Soviet society, a dynamic and more modern society has been emerging that does not readily submit to state control. In sum, by the mid-1980s, a limited civil society was born that Moshe Levin has described as

> the aggregate of network of institutions that either exist and act independently of the state or are official organizations capable of developing their own, spontaneous views on national or local issues and then imposing these views on their members, on small groups and, finally, on the authorities. These social complexes do not necessarily oppose the state, but exist in contrast to outright state organisms and enjoy a certain degree of autonomy.[9]

In other words, when Gorbachev announced in June 1986 that "Soviet society was ripe for change," he was merely acknowledging a fait accompli. Nevertheless, before Gorbachev's liberalization achieved some strength, the creation of unsanctioned groups with specific sociopolitical goals, especially human rights groups and nationalist movements, almost inevitably continued to provoke persecution of the members. It was only in the years 1986 and 1987 that members of informal groups emerged from the underground into the open and started actively participating in the public life of the USSR.

Why Unofficial Groups Grow So Rapidly

The liberalization of the Soviet political climate under Gorbachev resulted in a rapid growth of the number of unofficial organizations. A survey of young people conducted in Moscow in March 1987 showed that 52 percent of young engineering-technical workers, 65.1 percent of young workers, 71.4 percent of students, 71.7 percent of tenth graders, and 89.4 percent of students at vocational-technical schools considered themselves to be members of informal groups.[10]

Simultaneously, the Soviet press began to seek an explanation for such a quick development of unofficial activities. In 1986 and 1987, the press attempted to portray informal groups as a youth problem. Since 1988, it had to admit that older people had also participated in unofficial movements.

In 1987 the most common explanation cited the well-known tendency of young people to try to distinguish themselves from others (hence, punks and hippies) and the dearth of leisure facilities in the Soviet Union, which forced young people to find their own amusements (hence, unofficial rock groups).[11] A frequent target of criticism was the Komsomol, the main official youth organization, which, it was said, had become too bureaucratic to respond effectively to the demands of youth or to channel their enthusiasm for social activities. According to an opinion poll conducted in 1988 among 2,546 Komsomol members, only 6 percent of those questioned admitted their active participation in the organization's activities.[12] Such a situation naturally resulted in the creation of unofficial groups with sociopolitical goals. In March 1987, *Pravda* reported that students from an institution of higher education in Moscow had created an informal group "for the vitalization of Komsomol work."[13]

As *glasnost* continued to develop, the Soviet press started to admit that virtually all age groups of adult Soviet people had been involved in the activities of unofficial organizations. Increasing the degree of criticism, Soviet journalists began to suggest that the appearance of informal organizations might be a result of shortcomings in Soviet society. The journalists admitted that the establishment of informal groups reflected a desire on the part of people to isolate themselves from the activities of official organizations. Although it duly criticized this trend, the newspaper blamed not the people themselves, but rather the social conditions that compel individuals to behave that way. The gap between words and deeds, the Soviet press admitted, soured many young people on officially sanctioned public activities, which they found hypocritical.[14] Specialists in unofficial movements L. L. Lisyutkina and A. D. Khlopin also observed that a "crisis of many institutions of industrial society" had been visible in all the industrially developed countries. Therefore, they proposed to compare certain informal movements (punks and hippies being the obvious examples) with their prototypes in capitalist countries. Both authors, however, were careful to stress that specific problems of the Soviet Union (overwhelming official control and attempts by the authorities to suppress dissenting views) make Soviet informal groups a unique phenomenon.[15]

The Soviet media reports on informal groups in 1987 and 1988 avoided mentioning the decreasing prestige of the CPSU as an additional reason for the birth of new sociopolitical movements. Programs of unofficial organizations set up at that time, however, did mention the distrust toward the party as one of the reasons for their creation. For instance, the program of the Moscow Popular Front, elaborated at the end of 1988 and beginning of 1989, stated:

> The Moscow Popular Front does not want to become a dependent, obedient and hopeless "supporter" of the Party apparatus in all its actions and mistakes. We are trying to avoid the plight of official Soviet public organizations—submission to the authorities' control, bureaucratization of work and dependence on Party and state organs.[16]

2

Chronology of Development of Unofficial Movements

In 1986 the Soviet press concentrated its attention on the activities of apolitical informal groups. In 1987, however, groups for the preservation of historical monuments and ecological groups emerged as the first sociopolitical organizations to participate openly in the country's public life.

In 1988, the continuing liberalization enhanced the role played by informal groups in Soviet society. According to the Soviet press, at the beginning of that year informal groups numbered approximately 30,000.[1] In October 1987, historian Roy Medvedev said that informal sociopolitical associations were actually "political parties."[2] Because these groups were then principally preoccupied with internal matters, such as recruiting members and establishing links with one another, this judgment was a bit of an exaggeration; in 1988 it no longer was. Indeed, in 1988 unofficial associations throughout the Soviet Union entered the sociopolitical arena in earnest. The movements became especially strong in the Baltic republics.

In the course of 1989, many unofficial groups joined forces to form bigger and better-structured organizations. The majority of the new organizations established in 1989 advanced political goals, and the popular fronts, imitating the Baltic models, were established in other Union republics. While the all-Union law on voluntary associations had still not been adopted by the end of 1989 and the activities of the majority of informal organizations, therefore, had no legal basis on the all-Union level, Lithuania became the first Union republic to legalize political parties other than the Communist Party.[3]

In 1989, the development of the informal groups proceeded very quickly, reflecting the speed of political change in the USSR. According to the official press, the number of such groups doubled compared with 1988, reaching 60,000.[4] But not only had the number of informal groups swollen—the nature of their activities had changed. Whereas in 1988 the groups posed a challenge to the Komsomol, whose prestige among Soviet youth was waning anyway, in 1989 some informal groups were able to challenge the CPSU itself. Indeed, their rise coincides with growing public unhappiness with the Communist Party, which had been blamed for virtually all the USSR's misfortunes.

By the beginning of 1990, it was obvious to virtually everyone that a de facto multiparty system had emerged in the Soviet Union. In view of this, the CPSU agreed to abolish Article 6 of the Soviet Constitution, which guaranteed the CPSU's monopoly on power.[5] The adoption of the all-Union law legalizing political organizations other than the CPSU has been continually delayed, however.

Apolitical Groups, 1986–1987

In 1986 articles began to appear in the Soviet press admitting that unofficial groups of various leanings existed in the USSR. The Soviet press initially focused on those groups whose interests were outside politics.

In 1987 the number of informal groups, as the youth daily *Komsomol'skaya pravda* phrased it, was growing as fast as mushrooms in the rain.[6] The Soviet press carried letters from young people who mentioned the existence of informal groups in almost every city and even village of the USSR. The most common kind of informal group at the time consisted of young people who were interested in music—mostly rock and pop—and who formed amateur music ensembles. The government attempted in the early 1980s to register these ensembles. According to the Soviet press, in the mid-1980s they numbered more than 100,000.[7]

Sports enthusiasts (usually soccer fans) constituted another very common type of informal group in the USSR. They attended all the games of their favorite team and often got into fights with the supporters of rival teams.[8]

There were, of course, punks and hippies in the USSR. In addition, there were groups such as the *Lyubery* (the name is derived from the Moscow suburb of Lyubertsy), whose principal recreational activity seemed to be assaulting punks and hippies.[9]

There were also many unofficial literary clubs (the majority of these were in Leningrad).[10] Some of these clubs appeared in the 1970s and the beginning of the 1980s and continued their activities under the new conditions.[11]

In October 1986 *Komsomol'skaya pravda* reported on self-styled vigilante groups in Pskov and Novosibirsk that fought against corruption and other forms of injustice. The newspaper published a letter from a youth in Novosibirsk who claimed to belong to an unofficial group called *Zakon i poryadok* (Law and Order).[12] The newspaper quoted the youth as saying that the group had already solved 53 cases of corruption on its own, without help from the investigative organs, and that 15 additional cases were in the works. According to the youth, the group consisted of 35 people. Similar vigilante groups were established by veterans of the war in Afghanistan, who had found it difficult to adjust to the corruption of Soviet life after returning from military service.[13] By the end of 1987, media attention for such groups faded as groups with clear-cut sociopolitical goals became more active.

Groups for the Preservation of Monuments: The First Active Sociopolitical Organizations

The Russian Federation (Russian Soviet Federal Socialist Republic or RSFSR)

As early as 1987, the Soviet press started to pay special attention to groups that were devoted to the preservation of historic monuments and the environment. The press focused most of its attention on groups of this sort in Leningrad and Moscow, but stressed that other cities in the Soviet Union had similar organizations.[14] These groups, especially in Moscow and Leningrad, seemed by 1987 to have achieved a well-defined structure and were organizations in the true sense of the word. Moreover, they had a clear program of social activities and sometimes political goals. From the very start, however, not all of these groups have been constructive.

In 1987 Soviet and Western press gave a great deal of attention to the informal group *Pamyat'*, composed of Russian nationalists. *Pamyat'* was founded in the early 1980s as a literary and historical society attached to the USSR Ministry of the Aviation Industry. At the time of its creation, the group advocated the preservation of historical monuments and improvement of the environment in Russia as its main goals. The society failed to receive much publicity for its work until 1987.[15]

Then *Pamyat'* became one of the most discussed movements in the Soviet Union. In May 1987 this society staged two spontaneous demonstrations in the center of Moscow and was granted an audience with the then Moscow party chief, Boris Yeltsin.[16] It became clear that the group's rather honorable goals of preserving historical monuments and protecting the environment were combined with anti-Semitic, anti-Western, and extremely nationalistic propaganda. Members of *Pamyat'* seem to blame the destruction of old buildings and the environment in Russia on an alleged international conspiracy of Jews and Freemasons. The introduction to an official declaration of *Pamyat'* well illustrates the group's position:

> The true situation in our country can be revealed with one phrase: "We've played around enough with democracy [*podemokratnichali*], and it's time to quit." Reasonable and healthy forces of our society, not having had a chance to arise, are yet again stamped into the ground. This nonsense with *perestroika* must come to an end. . . . It is becoming clearer every day that enemies have imbedded themselves in every link of the Party chain, the governing force of the USSR. Dark elements in the Party, exploiting Party slogans and phraseology, are practically waging a war against the endemic population of the country and are destroying the national image of the people. They are resurrecting Trotskyism, in order to discredit socialism, in order to sow chaos in the government, in order to open the floodgates to Western capitalism and ideology.[17]

In 1988 the activities of *Pamyat'* had further increased. Whereas in 1987 members of the group staged only a couple of demonstrations in Moscow, in 1988 they held regular meetings in the Leningrad Rumyantsev Garden near the Academy of Arts and the Leningrad University building.[18] It also became obvious that some of the most conservative representatives of the party and state apparatus have sympathized with the organization. Indeed, in 1988 representatives of the Leningrad Oblast Party organization reportedly attended the group's gatherings; significantly, an opinion poll on the attitude toward informal groups conducted in Leningrad in June 1988 showed that the majority of party officials expressed no sympathy for unofficial organizations in the city except for Russian nationalist ones.[19]

By the beginning of 1989, however, it was obvious that despite a lot of noise created by *Pamyat'* and a number of other extreme Russian nationalist organizations, they did not enjoy the support of the general public. Elections to the USSR Congress of People's Deputies in the spring of 1989 and the 1990 parliamentary elections in the RSFSR, which are discussed in a separate chapter, illustrate this point.[20] The main reasons for the distrust that voters demonstrated toward extreme Russian nationalists during the elections seem to be their strong anti-Western views, their emphasis on the need to isolate Russia from the outside world, as well as their obvious links with Stalinists and discredited conservative party officials.

Of course, not all of the groups for the preservation of monuments in the Russian Federation turn into *Pamyat'*-type organizations. For instance, in 1987 several groups in Leningrad attracted attention precisely for trying to disassociate themselves from *Pamyat'* and for denouncing attempts to blame misfortunes of the USSR on the Jews. For this reason, these groups received positive coverage in the liberal Soviet newspapers, including *Izvestia* and *Literaturnaya gazeta*.[21] Among informal liberal cultural groups in Leningrad are "Spasenie" (Salvation), "Mir" (Peace), and "Sovet ekologii kul'tury" (Council of Cultural Ecology), which in early 1987 staged a demonstration in Leningrad protesting the decision of local authorities to demolish the hotel "Angleterre," where the Russian poet Sergei Esenin committed suicide in 1925. Members of the groups received an audience with officials of the Leningrad City Council and the Oblast Party Committee. Architect Aleksei Kovalev, the best-known activist of the Leningrad movement (at the time he was head of "Spasenie" and a leading member of "Sovet ekologii kul'tury"), signed an article protesting the demolition of the "Angleterre," together with such leading Leningrad cultural figures and scholars as academician Dmitrii Likhachev. The protest was printed in the newspaper *Stroitel'naya gazeta*, which officially identified Kovalev as a member of the Council of Cultural Ecology.[22] In their turn, *Izvestia* and *Literaturnaya gazeta* warned officials in Leningrad not to take repressive actions against members of liberally oriented groups for the preservation of monuments.[23]

Non-Russian Union Republics

Ecological groups and groups dealing with the preservation of historical monuments in the Union republics sharply increased their activities in 1988—that is, a year later than similar groups in Leningrad. The "Ukrainian Culturological Club" in Kiev, and the "Ukrainian Association of Independent Creative Intelligentsia" in Kiev and Lvov held many meetings in 1988. *Talaka*, in Minsk, advocated giving official status to the Belorussian language, wanted to increase the number of Belorussian schools, and campaigned for the preservation of the Belorussian cultural heritage.[24]

The creation of the unofficial ecological movement received additional inspiration from the disastrous consequences of the Chernobyl' accident. Therefore, the Ukrainian ecological movement *Zelenyi Svit* became one of the largest in the Soviet Union.

The activities of informal groups in the republics, including those involved in the preservation of historical monuments and the environment, tended to be more politicized than the activities of similar groups in the RSFSR. The preservation of the Russian cultural heritage was traditionally viewed by the authorities with far less suspicion than similar activity on the part of unofficial groups in the Union republics, where concern about national or cultural issues was often regarded by the authorities as undesirable nationalism. In 1988 some local officials in the Union republics were continuing to follow this trend.[25]

Popular Fronts

In 1987, the attitude of the authorities toward informal groups, although more tolerant than before the advent of *glasnost*, was still very mixed. Realizing that informal groups were here to stay, the authorities in 1987 made various crude attempts to bring them under official control. These attempts, of course, met with resistance, because establishing official jurisdiction over the groups would have ended their freedom, independence, and spontaneity—their entire raison d'être. The Komsomol was regarded in 1987 as the main organ for establishing control.[26] This did not turn out to be very successful, however, because many of the groups came into being precisely because young people could not find an outlet for their energies within the framework of the Komsomol.[27]

In 1988 the authorities finally seemed to have recognized the ineffectiveness of their previous attempts to channel the activities of informal groups in desirable directions, and they have sought to establish cooperation with unofficial activists in the form of a popular front. Leading jurists (most notably, Boris Kurashvili of the Institute of State and Law) and sociologists, including academician Tat'yana Zaslavskaya, have played an important role in this new initiative, together with the leading activist in the Moscow informal movement, Boris Kagarlitsky.[28]

The idea of the front was first made public by Kurashvili. Writing in *Sovetskaya molodezh'* in April 1988, he proposed the formation of a "Popular Front in Support of *Perestroika*" to unite all socially active people—that is, members of informal groups and individuals (both party and nonparty members). Kurashvili stressed that the front should not be regarded as a second party in the Soviet Union (that is, the CPSU would still have control) but that it should fulfill some of the functions characteristic to opposition parties—namely, to monitor and criticize the government and party apparatus and to ensure that they efficiently execute their duties. He also said that representatives of informal groups in the front should have the opportunity to express their ideas and requests to the authorities. Kurashvili insisted that the front should unite people from different, even opposing, groups. Asked specifically about members of extremist groups such as *Pamyat'*, Kurashvili said that such groups should not be excluded if they displayed an interest in participating in the work of the front.

It is probable that, before the idea of the front was publicized, a sociological study was conducted showing that the majority of members of socially and politically active informal groups at the time placed great hope in Gorbachev's reforms and were ready to cooperate with the present Soviet leadership. Those who rejected the idea of any form of cooperation or compromise with the authorities, such as the Moscow Democratic Union, which was created in 1988 by former dissidents as a party in opposition to the CPSU, would find themselves, it was believed, in a minority if an umbrella organization for informal groups were created. Indeed, many informal groups in Moscow and Leningrad at the time criticized the Democratic Union for its unconditional opposition to Gorbachev's leadership.[29]

The most successful responses to the idea of a popular front were the activities of the popular fronts in the Baltic republics. Not only did these fronts attract an extremely wide membership as early as 1988, but they have also received the support of the republics' party authorities. The inaugural congresses of the Estonian and Latvian popular fronts, as well as of the Lithuanian Restructuring Movement, *Sajudis*, were attended and addressed by top party and government officials.[30] On September 13, 1988, Reuters reported that Estonian artist, Enn Poldroos, a leading member of the Estonian Popular Front, was elected a candidate member of the Bureau of the Central Committee of the Estonian Communist Party. This was the first case of a popular front leader entering the ruling bodies, to be followed soon by numerous other similar cases.

The initial programs of the Baltic popular fronts were similar to one another. They were much more modest in their goals than those of the parties of national independence in the area, as, for instance, the Party of National Independence of Estonia and the Lithuanian Freedom League.[31] The programs of the Baltic popular fronts deserve special attention because they have served as a model for the programs of almost all of the country's major sociopolitical organizations.[32]

The programs demanded a guarantee of state sovereignty and the equality of rights of the republics in accordance with Leninist principles of federation, as well as a guarantee of the real right of nations to self-determination. In the economic sphere, the programs stipulated introducing republican economic accountability and an orientation toward various forms of ownership—cooperative, shared, state, and private.

In the sphere of national policy, all forms of the expression of national self-consciousness and national dignity were recognized as natural values. Goals were being specified that guaranteed the national minorities living in a particular republic the right to express their national self-consciousness in public and to encourage the development of their culture, literature, and language.

In the sphere of religious life, the programs stipulated extending identical rights to believers and atheists and ending state financing of atheist activity. In the cultural sphere, the programs suggested introducing a national system of education in accordance with historical and cultural tradition, the revival of national dialects, the return of immemorial names to towns and streets, and other measures to ensure the integrity and preservation of national culture.

Finally, in their initial programs the Baltic popular fronts emphasized their intention to cooperate with the party and government in implementing *perestroika* and denied that they had any plans to function as unofficial opposition groups. Although some members of the popular fronts in the Baltic republics favored at the time of their creation the separation of these republics from the Soviet Union, such proposals were not included in the programs adopted by the fronts at their inaugural congresses.

Within a few months, however, the logic of events and pressure from below made such a stance infeasible. The movements gradually adopted more radical positions and began to set the tone for public life in the republics.

Indeed, several of the most important proposals of the fronts' programs later were passed into law in the Baltics and other republics and have been endorsed—albeit reluctantly—by the central Soviet leadership. Examples are the Baltic fronts' ideas about republican economic autonomy and republican language laws. In 1989 the fronts also pioneered in drafting amendments to the constitutions of the Baltic republics, although not all of their suggestions were ultimately accepted by the republican parliaments.[33]

During 1989, the popular fronts further developed their position toward the political status of their republics and changed the goal of sovereignty into that of complete independence. The process of radicalization occurred most rapidly within the Lithuanian Restructuring Movement, *Sajudis*. Then, on December 15, 1989, leading members of the Estonian Popular Front announced the formation of the Estonian Social Democratic Independence Party. Its platform said the new party's goal was to establish an independent and democratic Estonia.[34]

Finally, in both 1989 and 1990, the Baltic fronts demonstrated their ability to compete in elections for popular support, which appeared to be much stronger than that of the Communist parties. In view of this, as the only hope of retaining some degree of credibility among the population, the majority of activists of the Baltic Communist parties had to announce a break with the CPSU and to proclaim independence of their republics as the parties' main goal. Lithuania became the first Union republic where the Communist Party basically adopted the *Sajudis* program as its own.

At the end of 1988 and the beginning of 1989, in response to the growth of ethnocentrism in the Baltic area, representatives of the Russian-speaking population in these republics started to establish their own groups. Calling themselves the International Fronts or International Movements, these organizations complained that the Baltic popular fronts, consisting mainly of representatives of the native population, failed to consider the concerns of the non-Baltic population. Strongly condemning the separatist mood in the area, these movements demanded that the Baltic republics remain within the framework of the USSR. The influence of the "internationalist" movements is limited. They are supported mostly by Russian-speaking workers at all-Union enterprises in the area, not by representatives of Russian intelligentsia in the Baltics, who generally support the popular fronts. The obvious link between the "internationalist" movements and conservative party officials and even neo-Stalinists in the Russian Federation further discredits these organizations.

Following great success in the Baltics, the popular front movements started to spread to other areas of the Soviet Union. Not everywhere, however, did local authorities react as positively to the popular front idea as they did in the Baltics. For instance, in the Ukraine and Belorussia, the summer of 1988 was marked by rigorous crackdowns on informal groups. The local press, as well as the central newspaper *Komsomol'skaya pravda*, published strong attacks on informal groups in the two republics, labeling their activists "nationalists." In Kiev, the authorities tried to place obstacles in the way of Kiev activists who in June announced the plan of establishing the "Popular Front for the Support of *Perestroika*." Similarly, in Belorussia, hard-liners attacked informal groups in the republic for entertaining the idea of establishing a Belorussian Popular Front.[35]

In 1989, however, the development of unofficial movements appears to have eluded official control, and one by one popular fronts gradually have been established in all the Union republics. In spring and summer of 1989 popular fronts emerged in Georgia, Belorussia, Azerbaijan, and Moldavia; in the fall of 1989 the Ukrainian People's Movement *Rukh* and the RSFSR Popular Front were created. In

1989 the Armenian All-Nation Movement as well as the Uzbek Popular Front had also emerged. By the end of 1989 Kazakhstan was also about to announce the establishment of the popular front.

Although the various popular fronts differed from one another in their goals and the means used to achieve them, they were similar in that they had swiftly obtained political power. The Azerbaijani Popular Front, for example, had quickly gained so much power that it started dictating to the authorities and organized strikes that paralyzed the economy of the entire region.[36]

Another major popular achievement for such fronts occurred in Moldavia, where the party organization had to accede to the front's demand for a change from the Cyrillic to the Latin script.[37] Moreover, on October 26, the authorities were obliged to grant official registration to the Moldavian Popular Front.[38]

Elsewhere as well—in the RSFSR, Ukraine, Belorussia, and Uzbekistan—the popular front movements are gaining strength. Although these groups are not yet able to exercise the influence of their Baltic namesakes, they can and do exert pressure on the authorities on certain issues. Salient examples are the successes of informal groups in preventing the construction of ecologically dangerous projects.[39] The independent ecological movement has also been very strong in Kazakhstan, where an informal group called "Nevada" was created to oppose nuclear testing.[40]

Commenting on the achievements of popular fronts in February 1990, Mikhail Poltoranin, a people's deputy and deputy chairman of the Supreme Soviet Commission for the Affairs of Ethnic Turks, said that at least in the Baltics and in Transcaucasia, popular fronts had become much more powerful forces than party and government bodies. Calling on the authorities to admit this fact, Poltoranin proposed an all-Union conference of popular fronts sponsored by Moscow. According to Poltoranin, an attempt to establish a partnership with popular fronts was the only possibility for party authorities to retain some measure of power.[41]

Informal Groups in the RSFSR

Apart from the aforementioned groups for the preservation of monuments and Moscow's *Pamyat'*, there are various other informal associations in the RSFSR that differ from one another both in the level of their tasks and in methods used to implement them.

In talking about the RSFSR, one should separate informal movements in the autonomous republics, which are part of the Russian Federation, from those existing in Russia itself. In its turn, as regards the specific nature of its unofficial movements, Russia can be divided into the Urals and Siberian region, the central Russian and Volga area, and Moscow and Leningrad.

Among the autonomous republics of the RSFSR, the most active seems to be the informal movement in Tataria. According to the Soviet press, 18 informal associations were already functioning there in 1988.[42]

In approaching the problem of informal groups established by the Russians, one should note that in contrast to various groups in the Union republic who tend to unite on the platform of their republics' sovereignty and cultural revival, the Russians have not thus far demonstrated an aptitude for consolidation. Indeed, not only has the RSFSR popular front set up in 1989 thus far failed to evolve into a major political force, but it also appears that there have been many controversies within the popular fronts formed separately in several Russian cities.[43] The only exception seems to be the Leningrad Popular Front, which claims to have almost 1 million supporters.

The main reason for such a situation seems to be that the idea of a Russian national revival is usually identified with chauvinism and, therefore, is finding it difficult to make any headway. Indeed, until early 1990, it was only extreme groups such as *Pamyat'* that had attempted to present themselves as the only advocates of specific Russian interests. Leaders of unofficial groups of democratic orientation have tended to ignore Russian issues, discussing democratic reforms on the all-Union level. The democrats decided to turn to the discussion of Russian issues only in 1990, in the connection with the electoral campaign to the RSFSR Supreme Soviet and local soviets. This development is discussed in a separate chapter. Here an attempt is being made to present a colorful picture of Russian unofficial groups from region to region.

• The Ural and Siberian region is characterized by strong Russophile traditions. In the words of the Russian nationalist writer Valentin Rasputin, "Siberia is the bulwark of the Russian soul." In 1988 the Union of Patriotic Associations of Siberia and the Urals was formed in this region with several groups close to Moscow's *Pamyat'* (for instance, *Otechestvo* or Fatherland in Sverdlovsk and *Pamyat'* in Novosibirsk) joining it.[44] In September 1989 conservative forces, including extreme nationalists and party officials, met in Sverdlovsk to establish one of the largest groups of this kind—the United Front of Workers of Russia.

Nevertheless, as in other parts of the RSFSR, conservative nationalists have been unable to monopolize the area, and in 1989 democratically oriented movements in Siberia and the Urals also raised their voices. Especially strong are an unofficial democratic movement in Sverdlovsk, a former power base of Boris Yeltsin, and one in Khabarovsk.[45]

• Informal movements of central Russia and the Volga area focus on ecological issues and regional studies. For instance, in Kuibyshev there is an active group of those fighting for the restoration of churches, whereas in Ryazan' one of the most active clubs organizes excursions to memorial sites.[46]

• Moscow and Leningrad are the main power bases in the RSFSR for democratically oriented groups. Their victory in the elections of March 1990 was overwhelming. In early 1990 there were reportedly 150 informal sociopolitical organizations in Moscow.[47] In 1988 these groups functioned more as discussion clubs than as political organizations. In the course of 1989, the situation changed, however. Thus, active participants in the discussion club, "Moscow Tribune," including academician Andrei Sakharov, historian Yurii Afanas'ev, and ethnographer Galina Starovoitova, in 1989 directed their energies toward creating a parliamentary group—the Interregional Group of Deputies. Within a few months this group had evolved into one of the strongest political forces in Moscow. Further politicization of the situation in the country resulted in the fact that in 1990 only those groups that dealt with current political issues remained the main focus of the Soviet as well as the Western press. For instance, in 1990 the Soviet as well as the Western media drastically reduced their reporting on the activities of the so-called Memorial society, which attracted considerable attention in the first year after its creation in Moscow in August 1988. The society's main aim is to collect information about and honor victims of Stalinist repressions.[48]

It should be noted that in Russia new unofficial political movements have demonstrated a different approach to the crisis of credibility of the Communist Party than did their counterparts in the Union republics. Whereas in the non-Russian republics, anti-Communist unofficial organizations in 1989 started to form a forceful opposition to the party organs, members of unofficial party clubs in Moscow have become one of the leading forces in the unofficial political movement by advocating a drastic reform or split within the CPSU. The so-called Democratic Platform, set up by nonconformist Communists in January 1990, is a case in point.

3

Activities of Unofficial Movements

The First Officially Sponsored Conference

In September 1987, several Soviet press organs carried reports on the first officially sanctioned conference of unofficial groups to be held in the Soviet Union.[1] The conference was held in Moscow from August 20 to 23 by representatives of 47 unofficial groups. The conference marked a significant step in the process of promoting public activity outside the framework of official organizations. *Moscow News* and *Ogonek*, two of the Soviet press organs that reported on the event, provided positive and relatively informative coverage of the conference. Western coverage of the conference was permitted to fill gaps in the Soviet reporting.

Soviet Sources on Conference of Unofficial Groups. The main subject discussed at the conference was the role of public initiative in the period of *perestroika*, and the majority of the proposals advanced echoed discussions on ecological, cultural, economic, and sociological issues that took place in the Soviet media in 1987. The main focus of the Soviet periodicals reporting on the conference were the proposals approved by its participants.

26

Moscow News reported that the participants advocated proposals to provide help to invalids and elderly people who did not get enough support from the state as well as to build a monument to victims of repression. The newspaper failed to mention that the actual proposal was to build a monument to the victims of Stalin's purges—a project that was discussed in the USSR at the Twenty-second Party Congress in 1961 but never implemented. *Ogonek* did not mention this proposal at all, but it did provide details of other proposals made at the conference. These included projects to support self-management at Soviet enterprises, to combat social inequality, to publicize juridical violations, and to democratize the USSR's electoral system. *Ogonek* also reported that the conference had called for an end to the extremist and nationalist inclinations of certain unofficial groups. (The participants had in mind the Moscow group *Pamyat'* and its branches in other cities of the USSR.)

Comparison of Soviet and Western Press Coverage of Conference. After *Ogonek*'s account of the conference was published, the Moscow correspondent of the British newspaper the *Guardian* met with the conference's participants and wrote a detailed report on the event, which included many significant details omitted in the Soviet press coverage.[2] Neither *Ogonek* nor *Moscow News* provided any background material on the main organizer of the conference, "The Club of Social Initiatives." (The club was created in 1986 to provide support for Gorbachev's reforms.) Although *Moscow News* interviewed one of the group's leading members, Gleb Pavlovsky, it did not mention the fact that in 1982 Pavlovsky was arrested for editing the first seven issues of the left-wing *samizdat* journal *Poiski*. He was sentenced in August of the same year to five years in exile under Article 190-1 of the Criminal Code of the RSFSR covering anti-Soviet slander.[3]

The *Guardian* also disclosed that Boris Kagarlitsky, who has a similar background to Pavlovsky, was also a member of the club. A member of an unofficial Marxist group, Kagarlitsky was closely acquainted with the compilers of *Poiski* and also participated in the publishing of the *samizdat* Socialist journals *Levyi povorot* and *Varianty*. He was arrested in 1982 and released the following year.[4]

There was also selective reporting in the Soviet press on the proposals made at the conference. The *Guardian* carried the full text of a manifesto of "The Federation of Social Clubs," which was drawn up at the end of the conference. Some of the federation's proposals were vaguely discussed in *Ogonek*, but neither *Ogonek* nor *Moscow News* carried the full text of the manifesto. Certain proposals, especially from a chapter covering the federation's aims "in the political field," were not mentioned at all. This applies, for instance, to the federation's call for a clear distinction to be made in Soviet law between antistate activity and criticism of deficiencies in the existing Soviet system.

The *Guardian* also reported on the proposals suggested by the seminar "Democracy and Humanism," one of which was to abolish the one-party system and to introduce political pluralism in the Soviet Union. It said that the majority of participants in the conference had rejected this idea. By contrast, *Ogonek* and *Moscow News* reported that the seminar's ideas had been rejected but failed to specify what these ideas were, and they also tried to portray the seminar as something of a black sheep among unofficial groups in the USSR.

The Soviet periodicals also failed to provide any background information on the seminar. This may be found, however, in the unofficial journal *Glasnost'*. According to the first issue of *Glasnost'*, the seminar wanted the truth to be told about the USSR's past and present and supported the development of democratic traditions in the country.[5] It called for the deideologization of Soviet society and for the abolition of the articles on anti-Soviet propaganda and anti-Soviet slander in the Soviet Union's criminal codes. Many of the seminar's members, such as Malva Landa, Valeriya Novodvorskaya, and Yurii Kiselev were activists in the Soviet human rights movement, especially during the 1970s.

The fact that the Soviet authorities gave permission for a conference of unofficial groups including former dissidents as participants represented a significant breakthrough. Commenting on the conference, the *Guardian* spoke about the rebirth of "independent *political* activity" (emphasis added) in the USSR. At the time, however, it seemed to be too strong a statement. Although it was clear that the authorities wanted to bring the activities of unofficial groups out of "the underground," calls in *Ogonek* for "informal groups" to place more trust in the authorities and in official organizations and to combine their activities with those of the latter indicated that the authorities wished to discourage unofficial groups from acting too independently. The selective reporting on the conference in the Soviet press was designed to downplay or even conceal the majority of politically colored proposals suggested at the conference and to hide the dissident background of some of its participants. This suggested that the authorities still hoped to channel the activities of informal groups away from politics and confine them to cultural, ecological, and social issues.

Unofficial Journals and Access to Official Media

During the campaign for *glasnost* it has become possible to find official press criticism of the shortcomings of Soviet society no less harsh than that contained in *samizdat* documents of the 1960s and 1970s. This fact has not, however, caused a reduction in the number of unofficial publications appearing in the USSR. On the contrary, the liberalization of the political climate has, by making independent activities less dangerous, encouraged the appearance of many new unofficial publications. In contrast to previous periods, the editors and compilers of today's *samizdat* periodicals are eager to bring their publications into the open. Some of the journals have been successors to *samizdat* publications of the 1970s whose authors paid for their activities with prison terms. Other periodicals that have appeared in the Soviet Union under Gorbachev are totally new and are being published by representatives of those informal groups. Indeed the distribution of their own periodicals constitutes the best opportunity for unofficial movements to make their aims known to a wide audience.

First Conference of Unofficial Journals in 1987.   The shortage of information in the official press about independent journals and the one-sided treatment they received led to the establishment of a special periodical entitled *Zhurnal zhurnalov*. This independent journal, the purpose of which is to collect and disseminate information about *samizdat* publications, was first published in Leningrad in December 1987. The Samizdat Department of Radio Liberty obtained the text of the first issue, which contains a transcript of a meeting of editors of independent journals that was held in Leningrad in October 1987.[6] The meeting was permitted by the authorities and journalists working on official newspapers and journals (*Izvestia, Smena, Sel'skaya molodezh', Avrora, Literaturnaya gazeta*, and *EKO*) as well as for the Novosti press agency attended the meeting. Nevertheless, the Soviet press failed to report it.

According to the account in *Zhurnal zhurnalov*, some major problems connected with independent publications were raised at the meeting. A number of speakers discussed the reason that, despite the greater openness of the official press, the number of *samizdat* publications had markedly increased. They pointed out that it was still too much of a struggle to have items published in the official newspapers, and frequently not worth the effort. In addition, unofficial journals discussed subjects that were still taboo for the official press. In his bulletin *Express-khronika*, for example, former political prisoner Aleksandr Podrabinek deals with the situation of Soviet political prisoners. The editor of *Vestnik soveta ekologii kul'tury*, Mikhail Talalai, said that, although his publication was devoted primarily to an issue that was covered in the official press (the preservation of historical monuments), it was sometimes the first to address certain problems. He cited as an example the preservation of cemeteries—a question that the official press began to discuss only after it had first been raised in his journal.

The granting of legal status to unofficial journals was also debated at the meeting. Some participants insisted that legal recognition of unofficial journals should be included in the new Law on the Press.

The issue of reproducing printed matter was also discussed. As was true of the *samizdat* publications of the 1960s and 1970s, in 1987 the majority of independent publications were laboriously typed with carbon copies. The Leningrad meeting emphasized that access to copying machines was still very difficult. (On October 2, 1987, on the eve of the meeting of independent editors, TASS strongly attacked the publishers of *Glasnost'* for using the printing equipment of a Moscow library without official permission.)

A statement made at the conference by Dmitrii Zapol'sky, a journalist with the Leningrad Komsomol newspaper *Smena*, provided a striking illustration of the ambiguous attitude of the authorities toward unofficial journals. Zapol'sky was at pains to emphasize that independent periodicals offered no challenge to the official Soviet press. He criticized unofficial publications for being superficial and one-sided in their treatment of problems. He also said that he had seen no discussion of anything really topical and exciting in unofficial journals. Zapol'sky did, however, speak in favor of establishing contacts between the official press and unofficial journals. He said that he would be delighted to receive unofficial publications in the hope of finding items worth publishing in the official press. His proposal proved to be little more than rhetoric, however, because he rejected all concrete offers. Aleksandr Podrabinek's offer to prepare an article for *Smena* about political prisoners—a

theme that would certainly be new for the official press—
left Zapol'sky very much confused.

New Situation in 1989–1990.   Two years after the first
conference of publishers of unofficial periodicals, the situation of their publishers has improved, although some problems remain. The majority of periodicals still exist without
official registration. (For instance, in August 1989, the
authorities withheld permission for the Interregional
Group of People's Deputies to publish its own newspaper.)
The cooperation between the unofficial and official press
was still limited in 1989 and at the beginning of 1990.

Some improvements were also visible, however. First,
the access to copy and publishing equipment of unofficial
publishers has improved, which has resulted in a dramatic
increase in a pressrun of *samizdat* periodicals. According to
the journal, *Sovetskaya bibliografiya*, the average pressrun
of unofficial material reached 20,000 copies in 1989.[7]

The situation had become particularly favorable in the
Baltic republics, where the popular fronts publish weekly
newspapers using official printing houses. (It should be remembered, however, that the access to official printing
houses was not a solution to all the problems. Because the
publications of the popular fronts were not part of the official yearly plans, these materials were printed at the con-
venience of the printers, who were in no hurry to complete
the unofficial work.)[8]

Another sign of improvement in the situation of the
unofficial press was found in the increased official recognition of *samizdat*. In 1989, for example, *Sovetskaya bibliografiya* carried an article by its correspondent A. Suetnov,
who called on major Soviet libraries to subscribe to *samizdat* periodicals.[9] He also emphasized the need to compile a
reference book on Soviet *samizdat*. Similarly, the journal
Yunost' in its November 1989 issue emphasized the value of
samizdat periodicals. Referring to a guide for unofficial
periodicals compiled by the information agency of the unofficial trade union SMOT, *Yunost'* disclosed that the

overwhelming majority of *samizdat* publications had liberal-democratic orientation. Although Marxist journals were occupying the second place, their numbers were three times fewer than the democratic ones.

Moreover, giving the reasons for the drastic decline in subscription for official periodicals for 1990, *Moscow News* cited among other things the fact that the official press was in many ways inferior to *samizdat* in covering events in the USSR.[10]

In addition, the access of members of unofficial political movements to the official mass media has also improved dramatically. The liberal periodicals, *Ogonek, Moscow News*, and *Sovetskaya kul'tura*, have become especially good in airing views of representatives of the democratic movements. In their turn, conservative Russian nationalists have monopolized *Molodaya gvardiya, Nash sovremennik, Literaturnaya Rossiya*, and *Sovetskaya Rossiya*. Since 1989, representatives of unofficial movements of various orientations have begun to appear regularly on Soviet television.

Outside the Soviet capital, the situation varies. Thus, in Leningrad, the television show *Pyatoe koleso* has been sympathetic to the local popular front, giving the opportunity to its leaders to address the city's residents. In contrast, the city's main newspapers, *Leningradskaya pravda* and *Vechernii Leningrad*, have been more supportive of conservative nationalist groups.[11] In Transcaucasia, in the course of 1989, the local media drastically improved their coverage of the activities of unofficial movements. In contrast, in provincial cities of the Russian Federation many unofficial movements still find it difficult to obtain adequate access to the local press and television.

A significant change surrounding the issue of the press and new sociopolitical movements will occur when new legislation on the press is adopted. At the end of 1989, the USSR Supreme Soviet approved in its first reading a liberal draft press law that allows unofficial organizations and even individuals to set up mass media. If this liberal draft is accepted by the Soviet parliament as a law, the majority of *samizdat* periodicals, at least on paper, will be granted the same rights as official newspapers and journals.[12]

Even this significant step, however, will not result in the transformation of *glasnost* into a true freedom of the press. Arguing against placing too high hopes in the press law, Leningrad critic Poel Karp is correct in stressing that "as long as most of the publishing equipment is in the hands of the CPSU, even if it won't be a ruling Party, a real flow and exchange of information will be only a proclamation."[13]

Indeed, the draft law on the press, while allowing new groups of people to set up media, does not specify either the issue of media ownership or the regulation of their revenues. The draft also does not question the situation in which the majority of media organs in the USSR and their publishing equipment still belong to the CPSU; therefore, it does not envisage the possibility of passing them to other groups or individuals. The lack of specifics could easily result in the situation where former unofficial publishers would still find it similarly difficult to ensure a printing base for their periodicals, even after obtaining official registration for their press organs.

Legal Status of Unofficial Groups

Although some informal associations receive official registration as public organizations, the majority of the groups, whose establishment was not officially sanctioned, have functioned in the Soviet Union with no legal basis as late as the first half of 1990. As Andrei Fadin from the Scientific Research Institute of Culture of the RSFSR complained, "It is only our rigid political system, created on the ruins of the NEP in the 'famous 1930s,' its hermetically sealed organizational structure, that leaves outside the framework of official life thousands of independent initiative groups . . . , transforms legitimate elements of the socio-political system into unofficial ones."[14]

During the past few years, several draft laws on voluntary associations have been prepared, with liberals and conservatives fighting over the drafts. In August 1989 a specialist on informal groups, Nina Belyaeva, contributed an article to *Moscow News* in which she gave details of the controversy over the drafts.[15]

Belyaeva disclosed that in 1989 the authorities (she did not specify which) came up with a conservative draft law on informal groups that was immediately attacked by jurists from the Institute of State and Law of the USSR Academy of Sciences. Quoting from a review of the draft presented by the institute, Belyaeva pointed out that it placed informal groups under overwhelming (and, therefore, clearly excessive) government control. The review emphasized that the draft failed to consider the situation in the Soviet Union, where informal groups were appearing almost every day despite the official attitude toward them.

Belyaeva reminded readers that the draft under review was already the second to have been produced during the period of *perestroika*. The first draft, which was drawn by the Ministry of Internal Affairs, the State Prosecutor's Office, the USSR Supreme Court, the trade unions, and the Komsomol Central Committee, was rejected in 1987. Although the authorities attempted to keep the preparation of the first draft a secret, members of informal groups somehow obtained a copy and organized several public discussions of it. It was decided that the draft was completely unsuitable as it was even more conservative than the existing legislation on public organizations, which had been issued in 1932 and which ended the voluntary organizations of the 1920s.

In early 1990, there has been some progress toward adopting the law regulating the activities of voluntary associations. In April a commission of the USSR Supreme Soviet held the first discussion of yet another draft of the law. Participants included representatives of the USSR Ministry of Justice, lawyers from the Institute of State and Law, people's deputies, and representatives of unofficial organizations. During the discussion, radical Moscow deputy Sergei Stankevich correctly argued that in the past two years some voluntary associations have been transformed into political parties. Therefore, a separate law should be enacted that legalizes the existing political parties other than the CPSU and regulates the registration process of those to come. After long debate, it was again decided that the draft law regulating new forms of social and political activities needed additional work. A special commission was established to finish preparing the law. In a clear sign that the authorities are not interested in speeding up the legalization of unofficial movements, representatives of these movements were not included on the commission.[16]

Problems with preparing the law on new sociopolitical movements illustrate the existing general situation concerning broad reform of the Soviet legal system. Indeed, the pace for introducing necessary laws is often too slow; adopted laws and drafts under discussion include both conservative and liberal provisions, which often contradict one another; and finally, as will be shown later, both the leadership and representatives of new movements often demonstrate the lack of understanding of what it means to operate in a society governed by the law.

Participation in Elections

By participating in elections, political organizations can measure their influence on and the support from a country's population. For unofficial Soviet political movements such a test was first made possible during the elections to the USSR Congress of People's Deputies in the spring of 1989.

Not surprisingly, the most successful performance in these elections was that of the Baltic popular fronts. In Lithuania, for instance, *Sajudis* won 31 of 42 seats assigned to the republic. Both the republican prime minister and the chairman of the Lithuanian Supreme Soviet Presidium were defeated by *Sajudis* candidates. Party First Secretary Algirdas Brazauskas seemed to have been elected only because the *Sajudis* candidate chosen to stand against him stepped down.[17]

Outside the Baltic area, during the 1989 spring elections, representatives of unofficial movements were cautious in their attempt to propose candidates. Although some representatives of unofficial political movements made their way into the USSR Congress of People's Deputies, in the majority of cases their victory was a result of their fame obtained outside the framework of unofficial movements.

A markedly different situation occurred during the election to local parliaments and soviets, which took place in some republics as early as the end of 1989 and in others in 1990.[18] By that time unofficial political movements were ready to compete with the CPSU representatives for power in virtually every part of the USSR. Unofficial political movements had also designed their own electoral platforms. Therefore, in contrast to the elections to the USSR Congress of People's Deputies, which could be described as a competition of individual candidates, the subsequent parliamentary elections were characterized by the competition of electoral platforms.

The preparation of unofficial political groups for the parliamentary elections is an interesting and important development in itself. Here it is analyzed on the basis of the material from the Russian Federation. In other Union republics, especially in the Ukraine and Belorussia, the situation was similar.

Independent Voters' Clubs.   In the 1990 election campaign, representatives of independent movements have shown themselves to be much better organized than they were prior to the elections in spring 1989. Because unregistered informal groups could not nominate their own candidates for elections, informals were intensifying their efforts to establish independent voters' clubs, have these clubs registered, and then nominate informal candidates through them. Although not all the clubs achieve registration, the number of those registered seems quite high. During the 1990 campaign, independent voters' clubs were set up in many cities of the Russian Federation to promote democratic candidates, whereas during the electoral campaign for the USSR Congress of People's Deputies, this happened only in Leningrad and Moscow.[19]

Using the experience of the previous election campaign, in the autumn of 1989 numerous voters' clubs in Moscow combined to form the so-called Moscow Association of Voters, whose coordinating committee included supporters of Boris Yeltsin and representatives of the Moscow Popular Front and the Memorial society.[20] Functioning as an organizer of campaigns in support of democratic candidates in the Soviet capital, the Moscow Association of Voters managed to get its own people into the official district election committees and into the Moscow city election committee. This was a significant victory because registration of candidates and the actual voting procedure depended mainly on the official election committees. The fact that members of the Moscow association were in these committees helped to restrict the ability of the party apparatus to manipulate the elections.

Similar coalitions of voters' clubs were also created in other cities of the RSFSR. To judge from available information, they were especially active in Leningrad, Sverdlovsk, Khabarovsk, Irkutsk, Novosibirsk, Tomsk, and Vologda.[21]

The trend toward unity was evident not only at the city level but also at higher levels, including the all-Union. The inaugural congress of the All-Union Association of Voters, which was attended by 169 delegates from about 40 voters' clubs in six Union republics was held in the autumn of 1989.[22] The association included voters' clubs whose members shared the platform of the Interregional Group of Deputies.[23] The connection between the Interregional Group and the voters' associations was not a superficial one. Upon its creation in the summer of 1989, the Interregional Group immediately emphasized the importance of the elections to republican and local soviets. In an attempt to prepare for these elections, the Interregional Group advanced a plan to set up a Fund of Deputies' Initiatives to finance the election campaigns of progressive candidates and to create data bases to collect vital information for conducting preelection referenda. The creation of the fund was, however, banned by the authorities.[24]

The associations of voters were not limiting their activities to the election campaign but were also participating in other forms of independent activities. For instance, the Moscow Association of Voters helped to organize a demonstration as an alternative to the official parade on November 7, 1989, marking the anniversary of the October Revolution.[25] In Sverdlovsk, members of the Movement for Democratic Elections were among the organizers of the so-called Civic Forum—a congress of about 20 informal groups in that city that gathered on January 16 to discuss the situation in the region.[26]

Leaders of Independent Movements Nominated as Candidates. In the elections in the spring of 1989, several representatives of informal groups—for example, Sergei Stankevich of the Moscow Popular Front and Aleksandr Obolensky of the Apatity Voluntary Society for the Support of *Perestroika*—were elected people's deputies. As a rule, however, informal groups in the RSFSR preferred to support leading reformers rather than offer their own leaders as candidates. The Memorial society, for example, campaigned in 1989 for the election of Yurii Afanas'ev, while Kharkov anarcho-syndicalists supported Vitalii Korotich and Evgenii Evtushenko.[27] Apparently, it was not only technical problems (the lack of official registration) that prevented many informals from nominating their own people for elections to the Congress of People's Deputies, but also the fact that informals were not sure their leaders were sufficiently well known to the broad public to obtain the necessary number of votes.

By contrast, in the 1990 election campaign, unofficial organizations were much bolder in proposing their own leaders as candidates. Here too, the independent movements tended toward consolidation. In October and November 1989 the most prominent Moscow informal groups set up the organization "Elections-90," whose aim was to put up democratic candidates for election to the soviets.[28] This organization for the first time brought together groups of both Socialist and anti-Socialist orientations, requiring only that they demonstrate their adherence to democracy. Thus, "Elections-90" united under the same roof the anti-Communist *Glasnost'* club and nonconformist Communists from the "Democratic Platform." There were representatives of the writers' club "April," the Moscow Popular Front, and the Memorial society in "Elections-90," which also included the social democratic faction of the Democratic Union—a small group within the union that agreed to participate in the elections. The Democratic Union as a whole was advocating a boycott of the elections, condemning them as a manipulative act on the part of Soviet officialdom. The Confederation of Anarcho-Syndicalists, whose members boycotted the republican elections but participated in the local elections, was also represented in "Elections-90."[29]

In Leningrad, a similar organization called "Democratic Elections-90" managed to offer activists of the Leningrad Popular Front as candidates in almost every electoral district in the city.[30] Because the Leningrad Popular Front was not officially registered, its candidates were nominated by registered voters' clubs and workers' collectives. Finally, in January, following heated debates, 158 candidates supporting a multiparty system and a market economy formed in Moscow the preelection bloc "Democratic Russia."[31]

It should be stressed that not only unofficial groups of a democratic orientation were actively preparing for the elections; conservative unofficial organizations also demonstrated remarkable enthusiasm. In December, a number of conservative Russian nationalist groups (including unofficial ones—the United Council of Russia, the "Unity" society, the United Front of Workers of Russia, the Brotherhood of Russian Painters, and the Union for Spiritual Revival of the Motherland) published the joint platform of their so-called Patriotic Bloc, which had as a principal goal the preservation of the Soviet empire. The bloc also criticized the CPSU's "betrayal" of Soviet traditions.[32] These groups created their own voters' club, called "Rossiya."[33] In Leningrad, "Rossiya," which received official registration, offered as candidates such odious figures as art critic Mark Lyubomudrov, teacher Irina Poluboyarinova, and anti-Zionist propagandist and head of the nationalistic group "Patriot" Aleksandr Romanenko—all of whom were known for expressing extremely anti-Semitic views.[34]

Platforms of Unofficial Democratic Groups.   In reporting on the 1990 preelection campaign, *Sovetskaya Rossiya*, which was traditionally critical of informal groups of a democratic orientation, complained that the electoral platforms of candidates of these groups were very vague.[35] A review of the available electoral platforms showed, however, that this was not the case.

The majority of democratic electoral platforms were based on the program of the Interregional Group of Deputies and included such broad goals as the introduction of a multiparty system, a free press, a market economy, and legalization of private property. But many of the platforms also included very specific planks that considered regional problems. Editor of the unofficial Siberian Information Agency, Aleksei Manannikov, for instance, promised in his platform to stop "rapacious exploitation" of Siberia's natural resources and demanded economic autonomy for Siberia.[36] The electoral platform of candidates of the Khabarovsk Popular Front proposed the creation of a Far Eastern Republic. It also dealt with such issues as the need for an increase in the salaries of people working in the Far East and for a more equitable distribution of apartments in the region, and even proposed establishing cooperatives to build garages for private automobiles.[37] The principal criticism that could have been leveled against the electoral platforms of the RSFSR's democratic informal groups was that they usually did not deal seriously enough with the general problems facing Russians, thus allowing the conservatives to portray themselves as the only defendants of the interests of the Russian people.

In addition to promoting their own electoral platforms, many informal groups were campaigning against the election of party bureaucrats to the soviets. The Samizdat Staff of Radio Liberty has amassed a large collection of leaflets warning the population against voting for party nominees. Among these leaflets is, for instance, an appeal to residents of Siberia by the Novosibirsk branch of the Democratic Union, which stated that one of the main aims of voters should be: "Do not allow the majority in the soviets to consist of deputies from the Party-state bureaucratic apparatus."[38] The leaflet emphasizes that the only party and government officials who should be elected are those who are known for their democratic views and ability to do a decent job.

In another anti-party leaflet, activists in the city of Berdsk (Novosibirsk Oblast) went even further, calling on voters to be cautious about electing not only party officials but even ordinary party members. The leaflet states: "If two candidates (a Party member and a non-Party man) have equal qualifications, the non-Party man should be elected."[39]

Party Reaction. Communist Party officials, in turn, employed a variety of methods to block the nomination of informal candidates. One widely used tactic was the above-noted refusal to register some of the informal groups and independent voters' clubs. Another was to allege that election laws were violated during the nomination procedure. A typical victim of this ploy was Vladimir Ivanov, a secretary of the Russian (*Rossiisky*) Popular Front, who left the CPSU on his own initiative. Ivanov had visited striking Vorkuta miners in the summer of 1989, had helped them to formulate their demands, and was proposed as a candidate by the famous Vorgashorskaya mine. According to the RSFSR election law, Ivanov, as a resident of Moscow, could be nominated in Vorkuta only by a national-territorial electoral district; but the chairman of the local election committee is said to have filled out the registration form as though Ivanov had been nominated by a territorial electoral district and then refused to register him on the "legal" ground that only Vorkuta residents could be nominated by the territorial district.[40] In contrast, according to both *samizdat* sources and the official press, when party-approved candidates were nominated, actual violations of the law on election procedures were ignored.[41]

Party officials at times used more sophisticated methods than just blocking the nomination of independent candidates. For example, members of party bodies were known to infiltrate unofficial voters' clubs to try to influence the choice of candidates for whom the clubs would campaign.[42] In desperate attempts to get themselves elected, party and government officials also at times showed readiness to set up joint electoral blocs with local popular fronts.[43]

Results of Local Parliamentary Elections. Elections to the local soviets held in December 1989 in Estonia and Latvia again demonstrated strong public support for the popular fronts. Similarly, in the elections to the Lithuanian Supreme Soviet in February 1989, *Sajudis* candidates collected the majority of votes, and the organization's head, Vytautas Landsbergis, was elected chairman of the Lithuanian Supreme Council. At its first session, the new Lithuanian parliament voted for the independence of the republic from the Soviet Union. The subsequent development of events in that republic was the most rapid.[44]

In Moscow, a preelection opinion poll indicated that the majority of potential voters in the Soviet capital supported the Interregional Group of Deputies (56 percent of those polled), followed by the democratically oriented Moscow Popular Front (34 percent). Conservative Russian national-

ist groups enjoyed little public support, despite the warn-
ings of liberal Soviet journalists that at least in Moscow
and Leningrad extreme nationalists, rather then party ap-
paratchiks, would pose the main challenge to democratic
candidates.[45]

The results of the elections in Moscow, Leningrad, and
several other Russian cities showed the correctness of the
preelection poll. The RSFSR elections were marked by the
victory of democratic candidates, many of whom represented unofficial political movements.

In Moscow, for instance, supporters of the platform of
the "Democratic Russia," drawn primarily by leaders of the
Interregional Group of Deputies, won 57 of the 65 seats
assigned to the Soviet capital in the RSFSR Congress of
People's Deputies, as well as more than half of the seats in
the Moscow City Soviet. Similarly, in Leningrad, candidates of the Leningrad Popular Front received the majority
of seats in the Leningrad City Soviet.[46] In some provincial
cities, members of unofficial groups also did extremely well
in the elections. In the Siberian city of Omsk, the entire
Omsk city council resigned, following the victory achieved
by informal groups in the elections. The conservative ad-
ministration obviously did not know how to work in the new
situation, in which radical informals started to dominate in
the city council.[47]

In a sharp contrast with the victory of the democrats,
conservative Russian nationalists showed extremely poor
results. Of the 70 supporters of the so-called Patriotic Bloc,
who ran for the same 65 seats in the RSFSR Congress of
People's Deputies, only two of them were elected.[48]

In Belorussia and the Ukraine, democratic candidates,
including leading members of the popular fronts, showed
good results in the elections. In the latter republic, the power base of the democratic candidates during the elections
appeared to be the West Ukrainian city of Lvov. Voters
there elected the chairman of the popular front *Rukh*, Ivan
Drach, as well as former political prisoners and long-time
Ukrainian dissidents Vyacheslav Chornovil and Mikhailo

and Bohdan Horyn. In April 1990, Chornovil was elected chairman of the Lvov Oblast council.[49] In Belorussia, the leader of the Belorussian Popular Front, Zenon Poznyak, was elected in the republican parliament.

In contrast, in the Central Asian republics of Turk-menistan, Uzbekistan, and Kirgizia, there were party offi-cials rather than leaders of unofficial movements who were winners. In general the informal movements in Central Asia seem to be developing at a slower pace than in other parts of the Soviet Union.

The victories of candidates of new democratic political organizations gave these movements direct access to one form of decision making, and they quickly made use of their new powers. In Leningrad, for example, the city soviet pro-ceeded to dismiss the conservative head of Leningrad tele-vision and gave permission for a pro-Lithuanian demonstra-tion despite the official ban on such gatherings.[50] Clearly, the new democratic soviets create an additional problem for Gorbachev's leadership, which further undermines its con-trol over the country.

4

Attitude of the Authorities: Constant Changes

Although in 1986 and 1987 the Soviet leadership started to revise its traditional policies in dealing with informal groups—that is, either to ignore them or to criticize them and harass their members—in practice many officials, especially outside Moscow, continued to follow old stereotypes.

In denouncing the unchanged attitude toward unofficial groups, Viktor Mironenko, then head of the Komsomol, complained at the trade-union congress in February 1987 that fans of rock music as well as members of unofficial rock groups were ostracized by official cultural centers and clubs in the USSR.[1] In 1986, *Komsomol'skaya pravda* carried several articles criticizing schoolteachers as well as Komsomol officials for ignoring the problems of informal groups.[2]

The Soviet police admittedly had been guilty on occasion of displaying a negative attitude toward members of informal groups. Punks and hippies came in for especially rough treatment, as did fans of heavy metal music, who set themselves apart by wearing unusual clothes. In March 1987, the Soviet press published a number of articles about a gang of *Lyubery*. The *Lyubery* claimed that their goal was to rid Moscow of hippies, rock-music enthusiasts, and punks. The press noted that the victims of the *Lyubery* usually failed to get any protection from the police. It appeared that the police did not protect punks and hippies and actually often repressed them as an alien element in Soviet society.[3]

Soviet newspapers also disclosed that members of other informal groups, whose activities would evoke praise from the authorities if they were officially sanctioned, had also been mistreated by the Ministry of Internal Affairs (MVD). In March 1987, *Pravda* reported that members of an informal group in the Far East that fought against illegal hunting had been severely beaten by poachers. For a long time the MVD refrained from initiating a case against the poachers because the group fighting against illegal hunting was informal—that is, not officially registered. In the view of the police, that was apparently sufficient reason not to extend protection to its members.[4]

Finally, the record of the activities of the groups regarded by the authorities in the past as undesirable in some cases affected the official attitude toward these groups in the first years of *perestroika*. An unofficial pacifist group, the Moscow Group for the Establishment of Trust between the USSR and the United States, set up in 1981, is a case in point. Its members were constantly harassed by the authorities in the first years after its creation. And as recently as 1986 and 1987 this traditionally negative official attitude was still apparent. In contrast, the activities of a similar pacifist group in the Crimean resort town of Gursuf, established in 1987, was received neutrally by the authorities.[5]

By 1988 the position of the top leadership toward supporting those informal groups, including sociopolitical ones that did not go beyond the perceived tolerable limits, paved the way for their members to act relatively freely in Moscow. In the provinces, however, the authorities often continued to suppress even those movements that had received approval from Moscow. One of the most tragic events occurred on November 1, 1988, when the police, on the instructions of the local authorities, used tear gas to break up a rally in the Belorussian capital of Minsk held to commemorate the victims of Stalin's purges.[6] The rally was organized by the Belorussian society *Martyrolog Belorussii*. At the same time, Moscow's Memorial society could freely organize its anti-Stalinist demonstrations in Moscow.

In 1988, however, even the authorities in Moscow were unprepared to tolerate those unofficial groups that challenged the predominant role of the Communist Party, advocated the separation of the Union republics from the Soviet Union, or rejected the Socialist system. Members of these groups suffered some form of repression in all parts of the Soviet Union, including the Soviet capital.[7]

In Moscow, for instance, the police attempted to ban all activities of the Democratic Union, whose challenge to the leading role of the CPSU was clearly unacceptable to the authorities. Apparently, the issuing of three decrees in July 1988 banning unauthorized demonstrations and stipulating heavy fines for those who conducted them was at least partly in response to the activities of the Democratic Union, which attempted to stage unauthorized demonstrations virtually every week.[8]

Despite official attempts to restrain the activities of unofficial groups within permissible limits, the radicalization of their demands and the increase of their influence have continued in virtually every part of the USSR. Together with the decreasing prestige of the CPSU, whose responsibility for crimes conducted in the course of Soviet history had become a focal point in the Soviet media, the growth of unofficial political movements increased the official alarm over the situation in 1989.[9]

Alarm over the challenge that the informal groups—primarily the popular fronts—started posing to the CPSU was first expressed by conservative party officials. Speaking in Moldavia in February 1989, Viktor Chebrikov, later ousted from the Politburo, called for action against groups with an anti-Socialist orientation and against those who take exception to the CPSU's leading role.[10] Later, at a meeting in July in the CPSU Central Committee, several conservatives, including Vitalii Vorotnikov and Egor Liga-chev, again attacked informal groups. Ligachev complained about the creation of "oppositional anti-*perestroika* politi-cal organizations with their own periodicals," because, he said, this had helped to create a situation of dual power (*dvoevlastie*) in certain areas of the USSR.[11]

In contrast, at the same meeting, Mikhail Gorbachev called for increased cooperation with informal groups, say-ing that the party had no alternative. A few months later, however, with the economic situation deteriorating and the Soviet leadership feeling increasing anxiety about the pos-sibility of the defeat of party representatives in elections to the soviets, Gorbachev had also sometimes lost his temper and attacked certain informal groups that he thought were helping to undermine the prestige of the CPSU. In his speech to representatives of the Soviet media on October 13, 1988, he described one of the most active and important informal groups—the Interregional Group of Deputies—as "a gangster clique striving for power."[12] In short, it ap-peared that at the end of 1989 the top party leadership believed that the increasing activities of informal groups, combined with sharp criticism in the press of the USSR's past and present, were contributing to a serious loss of prestige for the Soviet authorities.

There did not, however, seem to be much that the lead-ership could do to control unofficial movements. Only in 1988, the creation of popular fronts had been regarded as a way of keeping the activities of existing informal groups under official control and as a means of neutralizing the most radical informal groups. But the authorities evidently underestimated how quickly unofficial groups, including the popular fronts, would begin to advance their own thoughtfully devised independent political initiatives and, instead of neutralizing "radicals," would themselves begin to make radical demands. They also failed to foresee how quickly the prestige of the CPSU would decline.

5

Challenges to the Policy
of the CPSU

The initial attempts to elaborate a sound policy toward unofficial groups that would integrate some of them into public life took place in 1986 and 1987. Apparently, the Soviet leadership then realized that it was impossible to eliminate unofficial groups and decided to permit them to exist under official control.

1986-1987. On October 1, 1986, a Soviet newspaper printed a proposal to establish special departments in the Komsomol committees of every raion (district) or oblast (region) to oversee the activities of informal groups.[1] It was also suggested that a special sociological center be established to study unofficial groups and to conduct opinion polls among their members to determine what their concerns were.[2] Simultaneously, upon the creation of the Soviet Cultural Foundations, this organization promised to try to make use of the activities and enthusiasm of the members of informal cultural groups.[3] In its turn, a state organization for war veterans, founded in December 1986, established as one of its goals oversight of informal groups of Afghan veterans.[4]

The treatment of the groups, in addition to frequently selective Soviet media coverage of their activities, clearly

50

demonstrated that the authorities were already attempting to encourage one sort of movement and suppress another. The Soviet leadership clearly did not favor the involvement of unofficial organizations in politics and preferred that they limit their activities to cultural, environmental, and even more marginal issues.[5]

All in all, the problem of informal groups in the USSR illustrated the tactics of the Gorbachev leadership. The central press, apparently reflecting the opinion of the top leadership, warned local officials against suppressing unofficial groups, which could be regarded as a sign of relative liberalization. It was clear, however, that the leadership hoped at the time to place all new trends in the country under close scrutiny and control. Unofficial groups were no exception.

1988.   In 1988, the main twist in the official policies vis-à-vis unofficial movements was the introduction of the idea of the popular fronts. As discussed in the chapter on the fronts, this plan did not work the way that the authorities expected. The attempts to keep unofficial organizations out of politics also have failed.

1989.   In 1989, the Soviet press openly admitted that political pluralism already existed in many parts of the Soviet Union and that in some places it was not the party organs but independent political organizations that held the initiative.[6] In view of this and considering that the situation seemed to be developing in a way that became more and more threatening to the power of the CPSU, party ideologists had again started drastically rethinking their policy toward unofficial political movements. The new policy included attempts to infiltrate party officials into influential informal groups to manipulate their activities from within.

Proposals from Novosibirsk and Vitebsk.   The new policy was discussed at two seminars on informal groups held at the end of 1989 in Novosibirsk and Vitebsk by ideological workers of the Central Committees in Kazakhstan and the republics of Central Asia, as well as kraikoms and obkoms (regional committees) in the Urals, Siberia, and the Far East. The seminars were sponsored by the CPSU Central Committee. As reported in *Partiinaya zhizn'*, participants in the seminars admitted that local party organs should intensify their struggle for the support of the masses in view of the growing threat from informal groups.[7] The participants urged party officials not to permit the situation to develop as it has in the Baltics, where the Communist parties are having to consider "how to operate in the situation of being in opposition." It was also admitted that the situation of the party organizations has become especially complicated in Transcaucasia, where the authorities have "lost orientation" and even refused to attend the seminars.

The participants made the following suggestions for dealing with informal groups:

• *Infiltrating Informal Groups with Party Officials.* This idea was discussed at length at the seminar in Novosibirsk by the chief of the ideological department of the Kemerovo Oblast Party Committee, L. Plotnikova, who reported on the success of local party officials in becoming members of unofficial committees of striking miners in the Kuzbass. Plotnikova said that only by establishing close cooperation with the miners through their committees could the party influence the demands that the miners addressed to the Soviet government during the strikes in the summer of 1989.

• *Creating Discussion Clubs.* Participants in the Novosibirsk seminar discussed the need to conduct a continuing dialogue between party officials and informal groups on ways to implement reforms in the Soviet Union. To this end, local party committees have set up discussion clubs that hold regular seminars in which both informals and Communists participate since both are equally entitled to express their opinions. Speakers in Novosibirsk have also proposed transforming the so-called universities of Marxism-Leninism, whose role has been sharply decreasing, into such clubs.

The latter proposal indicates that party organizations are attempting to use informal groups to preserve some party institutions whose role under the present conditions is unclear, such as that of the universities of Marxism-Leninism.

• *Establishing Special Departments to Study Informals.* At the Novosibirsk seminar, the participants revealed that, to better analyze informal groups, special departments have been created in local party organizations, whose employees analyze the membership, platforms, and tactics of independent organizations in their regions.

An example of what such departments do is a report on the activities of informal groups in the Murmansk Oblast that reached the West through *samizdat* channels.[8] The report was prepared by the House of Political Education attached to the Murmansk Oblast Party Committee and describes the situation as of July 1, 1989. Using a sociological study, the report says that the majority of members of the local informal organizations are in their thirties and are nonparty members; only 20 percent are Communists and only 12 percent are Komsomol members. The report also says that platforms of the local informal groups are under the strong influence of the Democratic Union and the Baltic Popular Fronts. Some of the groups (it was not revealed how many) are similar to *Pamyat'*.

The most important chapter in the report deals with the attitude of local Communists and informal activists toward one another. The report says that the two are "critical and suspicious of one another." Only 12 percent of the Communists positively evaluated informal groups, compared with 67 percent of the informals themselves. Whereas 70 percent of the Communists specified that their attitude toward informal groups depends on the groups' goals, only 30 percent of the informals themselves felt it necessary to make such a clarification.

Intriguingly, the same poll shows that the attitude toward party authorities among informals and rank-and-file Communists is actually rather similar, which underscores the party's low prestige. Indeed, according to the poll, 60 percent of informals and 41 percent of Communists described the authority of local party cells at their places of work as weak. On the question of whether the prestige of Communists has increased during *perestroika*, 78 percent of informals responded negatively and only 2 percent positively. The answers of the Communists were similar—69 percent responded negatively and only 5 percent positively.

All in all, the report on the informals prepared by the Murmansk Obkom provided a much more thorough analysis of the situation of informal groups than had been achieved by the central Soviet press at the time. Indeed, in the summer of 1989 the central press was still not prepared to publish opinion polls on the various aspects of the activities of the informals.

• *Soliciting More Help from Scholars.* Participants in the Novosibirsk seminar also called for Soviet scholars— historians, political scientists, philosophers, economists, and ecologists—to assist party officials in analyzing the platforms of informal groups.

It should be said that the CPSU Central Committee has for some time been commissioning detailed analyses of the informal movement from Moscow's think-tank institutes. One such report on informal groups was presented to the CPSU CC (Central Committee) by the Institute of the International Workers' Movement of the USSR Academy of Sciences at the beginning of 1989. Written by L. L. Lisyutkina and A. D. Khlopin, the report describes the situation as it was in 1988.[9] It focused primarily on the emergence of such groups and devoted almost as much space to apolitical informal groups of punks and hippies as to sociopolitical informal groups such as the Moscow Popular Front. The report almost completely ignored informal movements with nationalist platforms in the Union republics, although in 1988 they had become quite active. The report thus seemed to reflect the attitude of the authorities, who at that time underestimated the potential of informal groups with political goals.

To appreciate how much more realistic the authorities became in 1989 about the role of informal groups, one should compare the report by Lisyutkina and Khlopin with a survey of sociopolitical informal groups prepared at the end of 1989 by Irina Snezhkova of the academy's Institute of Ethnography.[10] This institute is now also reportedly involved in drafting recommendations for the Soviet leadership concerning unofficial organizations, whose orientation toward national goals is growing. Wasting no time on punks and hippies, Snezhkova dealt only with political informal groups and presented the best survey and classification of these groups that had appeared in the Soviet press. Without any attempt to divide informal groups into positive and negative categories, Snezhkova assessed their role in various regions of the Soviet Union and showed where they posed a real threat to the authority of the CPSU and where so far they did not. Her survey also gave the best classification of informal groups in the RSFSR and indicated the likely trends in their future development. Snezhkova's survey thus provided a much more sophisticated basis upon which the authorities could rely in formulating an official policy toward informal groups.

Despite this growing sophistication, many party organizations have not been prepared to work under a multiparty system. Local party ideologists, speaking at the seminars, may thus be correct in arguing that the only possibility for party organizations is to attempt to make informal groups political allies rather than parties whose platforms are opposed to the CPSU.[11] The prospects for the party's success in this endeavor are, however, not good.

6

Case Studies: Political Groups in Moscow and Leningrad

Democratic Union: Moscow's First
Self-Proclaimed Oppositional Party

In the wake of intensified debate in the Soviet press about possible political changes in the USSR, representatives of several informal groups created a so-called Democratic Union in May 1988. The Union became the first organization in Moscow openly to proclaim itself in opposition to the CPSU, whose members subsequently were not immediately arrested by the authorities. The Democratic Union called for a multiparty system in the USSR and for the withdrawal of Soviet troops from Eastern Europe, western Ukraine, and the Baltic states.

According to Western agencies, more than 100 representatives of informal groups from various cities in the Soviet Union gathered in Moscow on May 7 to open an inaugural conference of the Union with the intention of uniting the informal groups behind a common front.[1] Judging from the reports by Western agencies, the majority of organizers of the Democratic Union clearly were people with a dissident background who were still criticized regularly in the Soviet press. Some participants in the inaugural meeting of the Union were, however, members of informal groups that had been tolerated by the authorities.[2] A special session to discuss the Democratic Union's political platform was hosted by Evgeniya Debryanskaya, an active member of the seminar "Democracy and Humanism" that was being attacked in the Soviet press for "anti-Sovietism." Debryanskaya was also a prominent figure in the Group for the Establishment of Trust between East and West, the official attitude toward which had softened a little in 1988.[3]

Speaking to Western journalists, Debryanskaya announced the Union's main principles, which did not or could not at the time receive any support among the Soviet authorities. The stated aims were the establishment of a multiparty system in the USSR; the adoption of a new constitution to replace the existing document, which made the CPSU "the leading and guiding force" of Soviet society; the creation of independent trade unions and a free press; and the withdrawal of Soviet troops from Eastern Europe, the western Ukraine, and the Baltic states, which the meeting's members described as territories "occupied" by the Soviet Union. The opening statement of the declaration of the Democratic Union stressed unequivocal indictments of the Soviet rule:

> The basic right of each person is the right to doubt, to search, to disagree with the majority, to err, and to defend his point of view. In essence, it is the right to be "against." We have gradually been denied these rights beginning in October 1917, until we lost them entirely, and this has determined the course of our history. In the name of an "earthly paradise," the Soviet State established a permanent purge. The more the regime murdered, tortured, and persecuted people because of their convictions, the more it lied about the coming society in which there would be no violence and murder. But the path of lies and crimes does not lead to such a society.

From May 7 through 9, the news agencies reported that the police kept a close watch on the meeting; some participants were questioned and even detained. The police, however, stopped short of making wholesale arrests and shutting down the conference.[4]

The establishment of the Democratic Union was a great novelty for Moscow. On the all-Union level it was not, however, because four months earlier, in January 1988, the Estonian National Independent Party was created, which also proclaimed its opposition to the CPSU. The creation of the Estonian group, however, was announced by a numerically less significant group of 16 human-rights activists.[5]

The main thrust of the appeal by the Democratic Union, as cited by Debryanskaya, was not new. Similar calls for political pluralism were made in numerous samizdat documents, including the appeal "To the Citizens of the Soviet Union" that was sponsored by the unofficial group, the Movement for Socialist Renewal, and datelined Leningrad, November 1985.[6] At the time this appeal drew considerable attention in the West. Moreover, at an officially sanctioned conference of informal groups held in Moscow in August 1987, representatives of the seminar "Democracy and Humanism" attending the conference called for the abolition of the one-party system and the introduction of political pluralism in the Soviet Union. Reporting on the conference, Moscow News and Ogonek claimed that the seminar's ideas had been rejected by the majority of the participants at the conference.[7] Both journals tried to portray the seminar group as something of a black sheep among unofficial groups in the USSR. The meeting, at which the Democratic Union was established, seemed to contradict the statement made by Moscow News and Ogonek. The meeting was striking particularly because of its numerous participants—more than 100 people attended.

The timing of the announcement of the creation of the Democratic Union is also worthy of attention. It came only three weeks before the Reagan-Gorbachev summit—an event that the Kremlin was reluctant to mar with a major incident that would reflect unfavorably on Soviet human-rights policy. In addition, the creation of the Union coincided with the increasing trend toward *glasnost* in political matters that became noticeable beginning in April 1988. Following the rebuff that conservative forces in the USSR received from *Pravda* on April 5, whose editorial criticized Nina Andreeva's infamous letter, the campaign for *glasnost* in the Soviet press entered a new stage, during which the possibility of political changes became the focus of debate.[8]

It was during this intensified debate over political issues that articles appeared by lawyer Boris Kurashvili, who proposed creating a popular front. Kurashvili and the Democratic Union may have had different goals, but the idea of a powerful umbrella organization for unofficial organizations was common to both.

Although the Union announced its establishment at the time of further liberalization of the USSR's political climate, it was immediately clear that the authorities would not permit the organization to operate freely. All of the main principles enunciated by the Union were at the time rejected by the leadership. While the proposal for a multiparty system was dismissed by Soviet official spokesmen as merely "unrealistic," the description of the Baltic republics and western Ukraine as occupied territories was condemned as "anti-Soviet invective."

Frequently during 1988, Evgeniya Debryanskaya—the host of the special session on the political platform of the Democratic Union—was detained or fined for participating in an unsanctioned protest against the abuse of psychiatry in the USSR, for demanding freedom for informal groups, and for other similar actions.[9] Debryanskaya also came under attack in the Soviet press for signing documents issued by the Group for the Establishment of Trust between East and West, which were described by the press as anti-Soviet fabrications.[10]

Later, the Soviet press continued to condemn sharply the Democratic Union as an example of a dangerous and anarchic force within the unofficial political movement, and the authorities continued to obstruct the group's activities. Nonetheless, the creation of such a large unofficial group

with such far-reaching political ambitions once again under-
scored the seriousness of the problem that informal groups
posed for the Soviet authorities.[11]

Politics in Leningrad and the
Creation of Two Popular Fronts

In 1989, the city of Leningrad became one of the centers of
intensified activities of informal groups. In June of that
year two informal movements were established in Leningrad. They were the Leningrad Popular Front, which was
set up by liberal Leningrad intellectuals, and the United
Front of Workers, which was set up by privileged members of the Leningrad working class and local party officials. From the beginning, these two fronts seemed to have
aligned themselves on opposite sides of the barriers, and
the Leningrad party leadership, headed at the time by Yurii
Solov'ev and defeated in the elections to the Congress of
People's Deputies, had attempted to use the United Front
of Workers to recover from its heavily undermined position
in the city.

   Moscow News carried a report about the constituent
congress of the Leningrad Popular Front, which was held in
the city on June 17 to 18.[12] The newspaper said that the
congress was attended by 680 delegates elected from over
100 unofficial pressure groups at factories, offices, and institutions in the city and in Leningrad Oblast. Among the
leaders of the Leningrad Popular Front were liberal intellectuals, such as Leningrad geologist Marina Sal'e, writer
Mikhail Chulaki, and specialist in political sciences Sergei
Andreev, who has written articles attacking the *nomenkla-
tura*.[13] *Moscow News* also briefly reported the creation of
the United Front of Workers, simply saying that its principal goal was "to fight for *perestroika*." This vague formula-
tion was one that various Soviet organizations, public figures, and party politicians were using to describe their
activities regardless of their real intentions.

More information on the fronts and their aims was given in the newspaper *Sovetskaya molodezh'*.[14] The newspaper reported that among the informal organizations that founded the Leningrad Popular Front were the Memorial and *Perestroika* societies as well as various ecological groups. All of these were known to enjoy favorable reputations in reformist circles in the city. The newspaper said that the Leningrad Popular Front was the biggest unofficial organization in the city, having upon its creation about 7,000 members. It also disclosed that in the elections to the local soviet in Leningrad, the city's popular front not only intended to support candidates with democratic platforms but also wanted to nominate its own candidates. The newspaper indicated that the popular front was concerned about the reactionary composition of the Leningrad party organization, whose leaders had failed to gain seats in the Congress of People's Deputies, and intended to influence it in a positive way through Communist members of the popular front. Such goals would undoubtedly receive a negative reaction from the conservative Leningrad party leadership.

As regards the United Front of Workers, which held its constituent congress on June 13, *Sovetskaya molodezh'* said that, although the United Front ostensibly claimed that its aims were similar to that of the popular front, there were worrisome signs about the new group. For one, the infamous Nina Andreeva was present at the congress of the United Front of Workers as an honorary guest. Unofficial reports from Leningrad, reprinted in the Estonian Popular Front periodical *Tartusky Kur'er*, also indicated that the United Front is against the introduction of a market-oriented economy in the Soviet Union and democratic reforms in agriculture.[15]

Leningradskaya pravda, the organ of the Leningrad city and oblast party organizations, gave considerable publicity and support to the United Front of Workers but not to the Leningrad Popular Front.[16] There was nothing surprising about this, though. As reported in *Sotsialisticheskaya industriya*, several representatives of the Leningrad Obkom and a first secretary of the Petrograd Raikom became members of the coordinating council of the United Front. By way of contrast, the newspaper reported, the first secretary of the Petrograd Raikom demanded the expulsion from the party of the one Communist for being a member of the Leningrad Popular Front.[17] (The Russian nationalist group *Pamyat'*, which was strong in Leningrad, was reported to have begun an agitation campaign against the Leningrad Popular Front, but to have done nothing against the United Front of Workers.)[18]

It is natural to question the reason that the Leningrad party leadership gave such support to the United Front of Workers. *Sotsialisticheskaya industriya* provided an answer. According to the newspaper, immediately after its creation, the United Front of Workers, together with members of the Leningrad party leadership in its ranks, advanced a proposal for changes in the election rules to local soviets. The proposed changes called for two-thirds of the seats in the city's parliament to be chosen by workers from major factories and for all preelection debates to take place at these factories. Members of the United Front of Workers openly stated that such a practice would prevent representatives of the democratic intelligentsia, including members of the Leningrad Popular Front, from being elected.

The Leningrad party leadership, of course, strongly supported the proposed changes in the rules. Being extremely concerned about the possibility of a defeat in the elections to the Leningrad city and oblast councils, Solov'ev's team, already having been defeated in the elections to the USSR Congress of People's Deputies, saw an opportunity for itself in the election-rules changes advocated by the United Front. *Sotsialisticheskaya industriya* even implied that the whole idea of proposing the changes in the election rules was born within the Leningrad party leadership and was just given to the United Front to promote. The Leningrad public quickly realized the trick, however, and on July 13, 1989, hundreds of Leningraders queued up in the center of the city to protest what they considered to be attempts to pack their city and oblast councils with conservatives.[19]

Another newspaper to report on the creation of the two groups in Leningrad was *Trud*.[20] The trade union daily clearly displayed its preference for the United Front of Workers, just as *Leningradskaya pravda* did. The position of the newspaper was not surprising because the All-Union Central Council of Trade Unions was together with party officials an initiator of the establishment of the United Front of Workers. *Trud* had a number of unfavorable things to say about the Leningrad Popular Front. Initially, it was clearly displeased with the fact that on May 27 those Leningrad intellectuals who later became organizers of the constituent congress of the Popular Front had held a meeting to demand the resignation of Leningrad party leaders who were defeated during the elections to the USSR Congress of People's Deputies. In addition, it was displeased with the fact that Western correspondents, as well as representatives of foreign consulates in Leningrad, were present at the Popular Front's constituent congress. Then, it complained that the declaration the front initially proposed looked like "the program of a new party." Finally, the newspaper revealed that it was less than enthusiastic about the fact that, at the time of the congress of the Leningrad Popular Front, representatives of other popular fronts of the USSR were in Leningrad and discussed the possibility of creating an association of popular fronts of the USSR in the fall of 1989.

In contrast with all of this disapproval, *Trud* praised the United Front of Workers for its appeal to the working people of Leningrad and Leningrad Oblast. Carried in *Leningradskaya pravda* on June 8—that is, on the eve of the constituent congress of the organization, the appeal expressed concern about the proliferation of "anti-Sovietism" in the USSR.

The clear disfavor toward the Leningrad Popular Front demonstrated by Leningrad party officials seemed to have contributed further to the antagonism of the Leningrad public for the Leningrad party leadership headed by Lenin-

grad Obkom First Secretary Yurii Solov'ev. The situation
became so tense that on July 12, 1989, Solov'ev was dismissed from his post at a plenum of the Leningrad Obkom
attended by none other than Mikhail Gorbachev.[21] At the
plenum Solov'ev was replaced by Boris Gidaspov, the man-
ager of a large enterprise who, in his first interview with
Soviet television in the capacity of Leningrad Obkom first
secretary, stressed the need to conduct a dialogue between
the local party leadership and local independent groups to
narrow the existing gap between the authorities and the
public.[22] Among those Leningrad groups with which Gidaspov promised to establish cooperation, he singled out the
Leningrad Popular Front and completely ignored the United Front of Workers.

In a few months, however, Gidaspov seemed to have
become influenced by hard-liners of the Leningrad party
officialdom. On November 22, 1989, he sponsored a public
meeting at which speakers reiterated ideas of the United
Front of Workers and attacked Gorbachev's reforms. On
the eve of the meeting, Gidaspov delivered a speech at a
joint plenum of the Leningrad city and oblast party organizations, in which he criticized the Leningrad Popular Front
and praised the city's United Front of Workers.[23]

Despite such support from the Leningrad city and oblast party organizations, the United Front of Workers did
not manage to succeed in putting into practice its proposed
changes for the election law. According to *Izvestia* of
December 1, 1989, the Leningrad city soviet rejected by a
vote of 385 to 16 a motion to introduce on an experimental
basis nominations and elections within factories.[24]

The subsequent parliamentary elections in Leningrad,
held in March 1990, showed that despite, or perhaps because of, the support on the part of the city party apparatus to the United Front of Workers, its candidates were not
supported by the public. Candidates of the Leningrad Popular Front, on the contrary, were the most popular among the
voters.[25]

Conservatives Consolidate Their Forces

During the summer of 1989, critics of Gorbachev's *pere-stroika* outside Leningrad followed this city's example and established their own United Front of Workers. Although these organizations have reportedly failed to gain much public support, the decision was made by representatives of various united fronts to set up an umbrella organization on the republican level.

The founding congress of the United Front of Workers of Russia was held in Sverdlovsk on September 8 and 9, 1989.[26] It was attended by a reported 110 delegates, who represented 29 Russian cities as well as Russian groups in Moldavia, Tadzhikistan, and the Baltic republics. The delegates proclaimed the same goals as the local popular fronts—the struggle against market-oriented economic reforms and the introduction of changes in electoral law to increase the representation of workers in the Soviet parliament. The delegates also condemned national movements in the non-Russian republics. Speaking on Moscow television on September 17, academician Andrei Sakharov expressed concern over the creation of the front, claiming that its program included points that posed a great danger to *perestroika*.[27]

Apart from serving as an umbrella organization for the local united fronts of workers, the United Front of Workers of Russia also expressed support for the Russian workers in the Union republics who joined together in various groups to protest what they regarded as the violation of their rights by movements for sovereignty and independence in the republics. Thus, the United Front of Workers of Russia from the very beginning was not a homogeneous movement, because Russian workers in the Baltic republics, Moldavia, and Tadzhikistan have different concerns from those of workers in the RSFSR.

The best-known of those organizations operating in Russian cities was the United Front of Workers in Leningrad, which was discussed in the previous chapter. Liberal Soviet newspapers and independent Baltic journals interpreted the formation of the Leningrad United Front of Workers as an attempt on the part of the conservative party leadership in Leningrad to salvage its position after the losses suffered in the elections to the USSR Congress of People's Deputies.[28]

In addition to conservative Leningrad party officials, among the founders of the Leningrad United Front of Workers were members of the workers' "aristocracy"—people who have traditionally enjoyed privileges, including high-level representation in the Soviet parliament. The elections in the spring of 1989 turned out to be a disappointment for some of them. For instance, one of the leaders of the front in Leningrad, shipbuilding engineer Anatolii Pyzhov, was defeated as a candidate for the Congress of People's Deputies after he said on Leningrad television that Aleksandr Yakovlev's policies had wrecked Soviet ideology. Pyzhov also accused Mikhail Gorbachev of deceiving the workers, because, he said, *perestroika* had failed to deliver anything to them. Pyzhov implied that only the intelligentsia had gained much from Gorbachev's policies.[29] It was probably not a coincidence that the first congress of the umbrella organization for the United Fronts of workers was held in Sverdlovsk, for there, too, the top party leadership was defeated in the elections to the Congress of People's Deputies.[30]

In an article on the creation of the United Front of Workers of Russia, Scott Shane quoted Arkadii Murashov, a radical member of the Congress of People's Deputies, as expressing the belief that support for the United Front was limited.[31] Party officials behind the front and its leaders from the ranks of workers, such as Pyzhov, were losers in the elections to the Congress of People's Deputies—Pyzhov received less than 1 percent of the vote.[32] The creation of the workers' fronts seemed to be an attempt by them to win back the power they had been losing since democratization of the country's political system began. In Solov'ev's case, however, this attempt failed immediately.

There was another indication in 1989 that the united fronts of workers did not have much genuine support among workers. The striking miners of the Kuzbass, whose mass movement started spontaneously and without the support of local party officials, made demands that were similar to those advanced by radical deputies in the Congress of People's Deputies and ran counter to those of the united fronts of workers.[33]

The movement of the united fronts of workers, however, could not be dismissed as completely unimportant.[34] This was particularly true because the creation of the United Front of Workers of Russia was only one element in the growing activity of conservative groups with a Russian-nationalist orientation. The day after the report on the front's Sverdlovsk congress appeared, *Sovetskaya Rossiya* praised another organization, the United Council of Russia, which held its inaugural congress in Moscow in September 1989.[35] (*Sovetskaya Rossiya* is a conservative newspaper, which dramatically illustrated its opposition to the democratization of the USSR when it published Nina Andreeva's letter in March 1989.) Representatives of the united fronts of workers in Leningrad and Moscow, and of the "Interfront" and *Interdvizhenie* organizations in the Baltic republics and Moldavia as well, participated in the inaugural congress of the United Council of Russia, with conservative Russian-nationalist cultural groups such as *Otechestvo*, the Brotherhood of Russian Artists, and the All-Russian Cultural Foundation. These organizations are led by such figures as the writers Yurii Bondarev and Petr Proskurin, the painter Il'ya Glazunov, the historian Apollon Kuz'min, the literary critic Vadim Kozhinov, and Mikhail Antonov, a technician—all of whom frequently have sharply criticized the current changes in the Soviet Union.[36] They have expressed their disquiet at the elevation to high positions and popularity in society—as a result of *perestroika*—of representatives of the Soviet intelligentsia whom they regard as left-wing.

Although often clearly bothered by what they consider a reduction in their own influence on society (Bondarev and Kozhinov were also defeated in the elections to the Congress of People's Deputies),[37] conservative Russian nationalists in their public appearances usually express great concern about Gorbachev's policies, which, they claim, are not in the interests of the Russian people. According to *Sovetskaya Rossiya*, speakers at the inaugural congress of the United Council of Russia were no exception. They suggested that the working class resist the current economic reforms, which would, they said, introduce elements of capitalism into the Soviet economy and thereby work against the interests of the working class.

The creation of both the United Front of Workers of Russia and the United Council of Russia signified a step forward in the consolidation of right-wing forces that openly opposed reforms. The creation of the two organizations indicated that conservative party officials, Russian-nationalist cultural figures, and privileged representatives of the workers, all of whom had reason to feel that their favored positions were under threat as a result of Gorbachev's reforms, were still determined to fight for power. To this end, they have appealed to Russian nationalism and have attempted to create divisions between the working class and other segments of Soviet society, especially the intelligentsia.

Democrats Attempt to Take Initiative on Russian Issues

Until the beginning of 1990, the conservative Russian nationalists associated with *Pamyat'*, *Otechestvo*, the United Council of Russia, and other organizations have been able to present themselves as virtually the sole champions of Russian national interests. In 1989, these groups joined conservative party officials who claimed that the lack of such institutions as a Russian Communist Party, a Russian Academy of Sciences, and a Russian Komsomol indicated that the RSFSR was discriminated against vis-à-vis the other Union republics. For their part, activists of a democratic orientation have tended to ignore Russian issues, often suggesting that there are essentially no problems that can be regarded as specifically Russian.

In the course of the 1990 electoral campaign in the RSFSR, however, the tendency of independent political activists of a democratic orientation to concentrate on general problems of democratization in the USSR rather than on problems specific to Russians was criticized by the democrats themselves. A number of items that appeared in the Soviet press in the first months of 1990 demonstrated that the democrats intend to rectify this situation. The fact that numerous leading democrats were elected to the RSFSR Congress of People's Deputies and to local soviets in the republic made drafting a more specifically Russian platform inevitable.

Analyzing the electoral platforms of various candidates for seats in the republican and local soviets, a *samizdat* author identified as V. B. Pastukhov, who clearly sympathizes with the democratic candidates, expressed his disapproval that "at a time when the national question is patently acute throughout the country, including the RSFSR, the electoral programs of democratic candidates are practically ignoring the subject. This results in a situation in which the chauvinistic approach has come to dominate the solution of national problems of Russia."[38] Pastukhov said that people with democratic views, if elected, "should pay greater attention to the national problems of Russia and start proposing and advocating democratic ways of solving them."

Simultaneously, the democrats themselves have begun to express concern that only conservative and chauvinistic forces have been raising specifically Russian issues. A declaration signed by leading representatives of the Interregional Group of Deputies, which was published in March in *Ogonek*, stated:

> We are concerned with the fate of Russia. Immoral people, who think only about their own interests, who want to separate the future development of our country from the development of world civilization, and who want to cause discord between Russians and other nationalities, have seized the right to speak in the name of the Russian people, in the name of Russia.[39]

In a clear reference to the conservative Russian nationalist groups, whose joint electoral platform advocating the preservation of the Soviet empire at all costs was published in *Literaturnaya Rossiya* in December 1990,[40] the declaration stated that "these people refuse to admit that Russia can become sovereign and prosperous only if it satisfies the demands of other nationalities for national revival. . . . "

Again, presumably in reference to the growing ties between extreme Russian nationalist elements and conservative party officials (such as Leningrad party leader Boris Gidaspov, who obviously seeks to play the Russian nationalist card to consolidate his own power), the declaration condemned "the emerging bloc of Black Hundred neo-Stalinists and corrupt bureaucrats." Apart from its condemnation of the existing situation, the declaration announced the establishment of a new organization, "Civil Action" (*Grazhdanskoe deistvie*), one of whose primary aims is to focus on the democratic solution to specific Russian problems.

In a similar move, Marina Sal'e, a leader of the Leningrad Popular Front, announced a plan to establish a Russian National Party.[41] In explaining her plan, Sal'e said that she wanted to create a party in Russia that would be based "on healthy national sentiment, not on extreme nationalism." Sal'e pointed out, however, that it would be very difficult to create such a party because Russian people had almost completely lost their national awareness. She complained the democratic discussion of Russian issues had lost ground to theories about alleged Jewish conspiracies against the Russian people, a specialty of such journals as *Nash sovremennik* and *Molodaya gvardiya*.

It is natural to ask which issues democrats regard to be specific Russian problems—particularly because they hitherto insisted that there were no problems that could be described as specifically Russian. Such problems as environmental pollution, the economic crisis, destruction of villages, demolition of historic monuments, and suppression of the Church are certainly not restricted to the RSFSR. Ecological damage has been far more severe in certain other parts of the Soviet Union, and the situation of the Russian Orthodox Church, for all the problems it faces, cannot be compared with that of, for example, the Ukrainian Catholics.

Some democrats have argued that, if there is one really specific Russian problem, it is for the Russians to surmount the vestiges of their imperial past and their subsequent tendency to regard themselves as "the elder brother" vis-à-vis other nations of the Soviet Union.[42]

At the beginning of 1990, in talking about Russian problems, it would seem that most democrats—especially those who have been elected to republican and local soviets in the RSFSR—have thought primarily in terms of limiting their concern about many of the aforementioned problems to the territorial boundaries of the RSFSR instead of treating them as previously on an all-Union scale. They also seemed keen to intensify their efforts to resist chauvinistic trends in dealing with Russian issues. As political philosopher Aleksandr Tsipko has phrased it, "There are two distinct processes taking place in Russia: democratization and the reawakening of national self-consciousness. If those two processes are separated, it will be very dangerous."[43]

In addition, those who advocate Western-style democracy have been gradually beginning to admit the existence of specific Russian problems other than the "elder brother" complex. An important one is that of Russians living in the non-Russian Union republics. Boris Yeltsin indicated a good grasp of this issue when, in a recent interview with the *Times*, he called for a law guaranteeing the right of ethnic Russians living outside the Russian republic to return to it. He wanted areas provided "where they can build houses for themselves."[44]

Democrats are still careful, however, to draw a strict distinction between the situation of the Russians and that of other nations of the USSR. A clear definition of this difference has been given by the Leningrad philologist Professor Boris Egorov:

> It is necessary to distinguish between the patriotism of large and of small nations. The patriotism of a small nation is a fine, unifying idea (think of the popular fronts in the Baltic). Naturally, no one is being stopped from being a patriot of a large ruling nation. Love for one's country is as natural as love for one's parents. But a genuine, innate feeling does not have to be flaunted. And loud, strident slogans about love for the great Russian people ring false, to say the very least.[45]

It should be noted that the democrats have so far outlined their new position on Russian issues only in very general terms. With respect to the Union republics, they stress a nation's right to proclaim unconditionally its sovereignty or independence. Soon, however, they will have to be more specific and begin to address certain technical questions— one of the most important of which is the terms on which the RSFSR should negotiate the economic autonomy of the Union republics.

Interregional Group of People's Deputies: From Parliamentary Faction to Formal Opposition

In July 1989, a small group of deputies formally announced the creation of the Interregional Group of People's Deputies—the first parliamentary faction in the history of the

USSR Supreme Soviet. Initially, the group avoided even the suggestion of political opposition, but by the end of the year, its radical members indicated that the establishment of a formal opposition was inevitable.

The Formation of the Group. As early as April 1989, on the eve of the opening of the Congress of People's Deputies of the USSR, radical deputies, mostly from Moscow and other regions of the USSR, met in the Soviet capital to establish what they called the "Moscow Group" of deputies.[46] Later, on the third day of the Congress, the economist Gavriil Popov unexpectedly proposed creating the Interregional Group of Deputies.[47] Two months later, the group convened its founding congress in Moscow and elected an illustrious group of cochairmen—Popov, Boris Yeltsin, the historian Yurii Afanas'ev, Andrei Sakharov, and the Estonian academician Viktor Palm.

The founding congress was attended not only by intellectuals from Moscow and Leningrad, but also by coal miners from the Ukraine and Siberia, collective farmers, and even army officers. The speakers rejected the idea of forming an opposition party, preferring to see the group as a parliamentary faction or a discussion club.[48]

At the founding congress, the speakers emphasized their support for Gorbachev's reforms, but urged quicker implementation of the entire process. As Anatolii Sobchak, a Leningrad lawyer, noted: "[We want] to stop talking about radical reform and start implementing it."[49] The writer Aleksandr Gel'man suggested that the alleged "radicalism of deputies, gathered [at the founding congress], is simply realism."[50] Another deputy, Sergei Stankevich, stated that the formation of different opinion groups, which would suggest alternative projects, was essential for the successful functioning of any parliament.[51]

The Interregional Group offered a draft platform that contained mostly well-known proposals, such as giving workers the right to buy their factories, ending the state's monopoly on television broadcasting, and introducing direct elections of the country's president by popular ballot.[52]

Participants also called for an extraordinary session of the Congress of People's Deputies for September 1989, which would consider constitutional amendments related to elections.

The organizers of the Interregional Group also addressed practical matters. They agreed to participate in the creation of independent voters' clubs, which would focus on elections to the local soviets and republican parliaments.[53] To this end, they established the Fund of Deputies' Initiatives, which was intended to finance election campaigns of progressive candidates and create data bases containing vital information for elections and procedures for preelection referendums.[54] The deputies also decided to publish the newspaper, *Narodnyi deputat*.[55]

Professor Yurii Afanas'ev delivered the most radical speech at the founding congress, criticizing Gorbachev and rejecting Marxism-Leninism. In his conception, the formula "socialism versus capitalism" had become an anachronism. Afanas'ev suggested that the Soviet Union had a long way to go before it could achieve the living standard of the capitalist West. As regards Gorbachev, he said that the party general secretary and the president "has problems understanding that he is no longer the only leader of *perestroika*. The leading role in the process of restructuring is currently played by various strata of society: residents of the Baltic republics; coal miners; and other social groups." Afanas'ev also called Gorbachev's attempts to preserve the status quo between various groups in society "an ugly phenomenon" that "prevents the development of political restructuring."[56]

Sociological Portrait of the Interregional Group. The group's "Information Bulletin," published on September 15, 1989, claimed a membership of 388 deputies (or 17 percent of the 2,250 members of the USSR Congress of People's Deputies). This figure included 86 members of the USSR Supreme Soviet (or about 16 percent of the 542 Supreme Soviet membership.)

Most members were Communists. Of the group's five cochairmen only Andrei Sakharov was not a CPSU member. In terms of demographics, a clear majority of the members came from the RSFSR (286), including 69 representatives from Moscow and the Moscow oblast. After that came the Ukraine (with 48 members) and then the Baltic republics (with 15 representatives). According to Viktor Palm, approximately 130 deputies from Estonia, Latvia, and Lithuania supported the Interregional Group, but formally belonged to other organizations. All the other Union republics, with the exception of the Turkmen Republic, were represented in the Interregional Group by at least one member.

As expected, intellectuals were well represented in the Interregional Group (with 133 members). In contrast to claims by the group's opponents, however, representatives of other social and professional groups of Soviet society were also prominent. In September 1989, there were 61 workers, 10 military men, 2 collective farmers, and 36 technicians. There were also reportedly 20 representatives of the party apparatus, Komsomol, and trade unions in the Interregional Group.

The Program of the Interregional Group. At its subsequent meeting in Moscow on September 23 and 24, 1989, the Interregional Group continued its discussions and produced a revised draft of its program, spelling out its aims and principles and outlining reforms in political, economic, juridical, social, and ecological spheres.[57] Although the consensus was that the draft needed further revisions, the group agreed upon some basic guiding principles.

The draft program acknowledged the popularly elected soviets as the ultimate source of state power. A new constitution, according to the program, would ensure the separation of powers between the legislature, the executive, and the judiciary. The chairman of the Supreme Soviet would be elected by universal suffrage. Electoral procedures were to be reformed so that local authorities could no longer control the selection of candidates. The group also stressed the need to eliminate the provision that allowed one-third of the seats in the USSR Congress of People's Deputies to be assigned to nominees of officially recognized public organizations, including the CPSU.

A new constitution, which was one of Andrei Sakharov's pet projects, would be the backbone of major reform. Article 6 of the current constitution, stipulating the leading role of the CPSU, would be eliminated.[58] The sovereignty of the Union republics would be strengthened, and increased national and cultural self-determination would be granted to autonomous republics and oblasts.

The program also stipulated the "de-monopolization" of the economy. Central control would be retained only in such areas as defense, for which it is the most efficient means of organization. Various forms of property relations would be permitted, and ownership of private property would be legalized. Full equality before the law would be accorded to state-owned enterprises, enterprises owned by or leased from the state by work collectives, and private or cooperatively owned enterprises. Market forces would play a greater role in regulating economic activity.

In the sphere of human rights, the Soviet Union would be in full accord with the international agreements to which it was a signatory. The program of the Interregional Group guaranteed freedom of the press and gave Soviet citizens the right to establish independent political, social, and professional organizations, as well as trade unions. People's deputies were guaranteed the right to form parliamentary factions.

The Attitude of the Authorities.   The top party leadership has reacted cautiously, and at times even negatively, to the formation of the Interregional Group. When the group was formed, Mikhail Gorbachev told the Supreme Soviet that he feared its existence would make decision making in the Soviet parliament "more complicated."[59] Later, in October 1989, Gorbachev leveled an even stronger attack on the Interregional Group, suggesting in a speech before media representatives that Yurii Afanas'ev, Gavriil Popov, and other leaders had joined party maverick Boris Yeltsin to form a "clique striving for power."[60] It seems that the main source of Gorbachev's antagonism toward the leaders of the Interregional Group is their popularity among the general public.

The chairman of the Council of the Union of the USSR Supreme Soviet, Evgenii Primakov, suggested that there was no need at all for the creation of the group. He proposed instead that deputies work more actively in committees and commissions of the USSR Congress of People's Deputies.[61] Gorbachev's deputy, Anatolii Lukyanov, however, expressed a more positive assessment of the Interregional Group. He said on Soviet television that he welcomed the establishment of the Interregional Group and considered it important that alternative opinions be heard when solutions to problems were being devised.[62]

Meanwhile, the Interregional Group was attacked by conservative members of the USSR Congress of People's Deputies and quickly became the main target of the United Front of Workers of Russia.[63] On the whole, top government and party authorities have attempted to hamper the activities of the Interregional Group. The authorities delivered a serious blow when they demanded the closure of the Fund of Deputies' Initiatives,[64] citing Stalin's legislation in the 1930s prohibiting the use of private funds for political purposes. The Interregional Group also failed to receive official permission to publish its own newspaper, and the authorities denied it access to official printing equipment. Therefore, the first issue of *Narodnyi deputat* was published under the masthead of *Sovetsky fizik*—the house journal of the Kurchatov Institute of Atomic Physics in Moscow.[65]

Gradual Move toward Opposition. Although initially hesitant to be considered an opposition movement, the radical members of the Interregional Group gradually have begun to accept this new role. Yurii Afanas'ev took the first tentative steps in this direction when he said, at the group's meeting at the end of September, that the Interregional Group was the only faction within the USSR Congress of People's Deputies that enjoyed a broad political base. He said that, therefore, the Interregional Group could begin to be viewed as a manifestation of political opposition.[66]

At the beginning of December 1989, five members of the Interregional Group called for a two-hour general strike to demand the abolition of Article 6 of the Soviet Constitution.[67] Although the call did not have much effect—when the strike was to take place on December 11, only a limited number of Soviet citizens stayed away from work—the call itself showed how frustrated the group's radicals had become over the slow pace of reforms. At a meeting of the group on December 14, Yurii Afanas'ev again proposed the creation of a formal opposition, which could eventually become a political party challenging the CPSU for power.[68]

Afanas'ev was supported by Andrei Sakharov. In what turned out to be his last public statement, Sakharov said, "I support the formula of opposition. What is opposition? First, we cannot accept responsibility for what the leadership is doing now. It is leading the country toward a catastrophe by prolonging the process of *perestroika*. . . . "[69]

Most Interregional Group members reacted negatively to this proposal, and Sakharov's sudden death postponed any decision making. Several days later, it became apparent that a split within the ranks of the Interregional Group would eventually occur, with the radical wing proclaiming itself in opposition and the moderate wing disassociating itself from the radicals.[70]

In 1990, leaders of the Interregional Group (including Afanas'ev, Yeltsin, and Popov) became members of the coordinating committee of another political force, which emerged as the most serious rival to the CPSU—the Democratic Platform of nonconformist Communists.

Democratic Platform: The First Step
toward a Split in the CPSU

In 1989, for the first time, the Soviet press printed information indicating that unity within the CPSU is a myth. Outspoken political commentators have argued that such Politburo members as Egor Ligachev and Aleksandr Yakovlev actually expound opposing views and pursue opposing policies.[71] Among rank-and-file Communists the range of opinions has also been striking—from Nina Andreeva with her Stalinist views to Professor Yurii Afanas'ev, who advocates rejecting outdated Marxist-Leninist theories.

In 1990, the Communist parties in the Baltics, with Lithuania paving the way, have also demonstrated that there is a split within their ranks. In the first months of the year, the majority of the Communists in the Baltics proclaimed their independence from Moscow, advocated political sovereignty for these republics as their main goal, and rejected "administrative socialism" as well as other types of utopian models.[72] Simultaneously, conservatives within these parties created their own pro-Moscow factions. In addition, some Communists in the Baltics and Georgia joined the newly created unofficial Social Democratic parties.[73]

As of the beginning of 1990, a split within the ranks of the CPSU on the all-Union level has also begun to appear inevitable. The first major step toward dividing the CPSU into Social Democratic and traditional Marxist-Leninist parties was made in January 1990, when a group of reformist Communists gathered in Moscow to announce the creation of a new informal group of party members—the Democratic Platform. The group held its founding congress on January 20 and 21 with 450 radical Communists from across the USSR in attendance.[74] The leaders of the new organization were young Moscow Communists Igor Chubais and Vladimir Lysenko, who in 1988 were instrumental in forming the *Mezhklubnaya partgruppa* (the Interclub Party Group), which later became the nucleus of the Democratic Platform. (The Interclub Party Group emerged in protest against the undemocratic nature of the elections of delegates to the Nineteenth Party Conference.)[75] Several highly placed Communists have also given their support to the Democratic Platform. Among them is Vyacheslav Shostakovsky, rector of the Moscow Higher Party School. Shostakovsky, who has come out in the Soviet press with radical proposals for reforms within the CPSU, became a member of the coordinating council of the Democratic Platform.[76]

The Democratic Platform announced its program, which included the following proposals:

• Article 6 of the Soviet Constitution, which stipulates the CPSU's leading role in society, should be abolished. According to the Democratic Platform, the CPSU should become a parliamentary-type political party.
• A multiparty system should be introduced, and the CPSU should have equal rights with other political parties in struggling for power in elections.
• The CPSU itself should officially permit a split into conservative and liberal wings. Various factions should be permitted within its ranks.
• The liberal wing of the CPSU should form a coalition with other political parties of democratic orientation.
• The CPSU should use only those ideas of Karl Marx that have stood the test of time and should reject everything that has been discredited by the history of the twentieth century as utopian. The Communist Party should be more open to the achievements of non-Marxist thought.
• The CPSU should openly admit its guilt for the "consequences of the totalitarian regime" in the USSR.[77]

The program of the Democratic Platform also devoted considerable space to the current crisis of the CPSU, which, according to the group, the party's leadership is not completely willing to acknowledge. The program stated that although the party leadership indeed initially gave an impetus to *perestroika*, currently, "the Party is lagging behind positive social processes [in the USSR] and is gradually becoming an obstacle in the way of *perestroika*."

It seems to have been a demonstration of good political sense for the Democratic Platform to have announced its existence on the eve of the CPSU Central Committee Plenum held in Moscow at the beginning of February 1990. This plenum voted almost unanimously to relinquish the party's constitutionally guaranteed monopoly on power and endorsed a draft of the new official platform of the CPSU Central Committee. Although by the time of the plenum the Democratic Platform had existed less than a month, some speakers at its sessions proposed that the Democratic Platform's program should be adopted by the CPSU as its own.[78]

The CPSU relatively quickly demonstrated recognition of the growing strength of the Democratic Platform. It seems to be more than a coincidence that on the very eve of the elections on March 4, 1990, in the RSFSR, Ukraine, and Belorussia, *Pravda* published the text of the program of the Democratic Platform.[79] In an apparent attempt to influence voters in favor of the Communist Party, CPSU officials, in their comments accompanying the text of the program of nonconformist Communists, stated that this program is actually very close to the draft of the new official program of the CPSU Central Committee. Party officials obviously felt it necessary to downplay the differences between the draft of the official party program and that of the unorthodox Communists. The differences are significant, however. Thus, Lysenko and Shostakovsky, also interviewed in the same issue of *Pravda*, argued that in contrast to the Democratic Platform, the draft party program does not analyze the current crisis of the CPSU. While envisaging the introduction of a multiparty system in the USSR, the official program still regards the CPSU as the most important political force in society—the force that consolidates social and political groupings. The official program, they complained, does not foresee a situation in which the CPSU might cease to be the most influential political force. Overtly critical of Gorbachev's centrist policies, Shostakovsky argued that the policy of constant compromises with groups of opposing political orientation is much more dangerous and unwise than allowing a split that has become imminent to occur. Obviously recalling the situation in Eastern Europe, Lysenko in turn argued that "if *perestroika* would have been brought to its logical conclusion," the Communist Party would have become just one of the numerous political parties operating in the country, not necessarily the most successful.

On April 23, 1990, leaders of the Democratic platform met in Moscow to form an organizing committee to plan for the movement's eventual transformation into a rival political party. Some leaders of the platform, including Yurii Afanas'ev, who quit the CPSU on April 18, and Igor Chubais, who had been expelled from the party ranks some days earlier, have argued that the CPSU is "beyond redemption" and is incapable of reforming itself.[80] They have advocated the creation of a separate Social Democratic Party that would include activists of the Democratic Platform and the Interregional Group. The idea of breaking with the CPSU before the party congress was proposed by some leaders of the group after the CPSU Central Committee issued a statement on April 11, 1990, accusing the Democratic Platform of trying "to split and even dismantle" the CPSU.

Despite the CPSU Central Committee statement attacking the Democratic Platform, the majority of its leading members still prefer to remain in the Communist Party, at least until it holds its Twenty-eighth Congress in July 1990. One argument is that it may still be possible to reform the CPSU from within; another is that the party congress will give nonconformist Communists an ideal rostrum to publicize their goals; yet another is that, if the reformers break with the CPSU before the congress, they will forfeit their claim to a share of the party's property. As Sergei Stankevich put it, nonconformist Communists should not "walk away from the Party with empty hands and bare bottoms."[81]

7

Conclusion

During the course of *perestroika*, unofficial groups have played a significant role in Soviet politics. First, they helped to democratize Soviet society—they became a channel through which many citizens have been able to express their views and become involved in the social and political life of the country. Using their *samizdat* periodicals, unofficial groups have undermined official control of the mass media. Some reformist proposals initially advanced by unofficial organizations were later adopted as official policies by the Soviet leadership.

In the past year, some unofficial political movements have evolved into political parties, challenging the leading role of the CPSU in society. Largely because of pressure exerted by these groups, the Communist Party agreed to abolish Article 6 of the USSR Constitution, which guaranteed the CPSU's monopoly on power. This development prompts a number of questions. Is the existence of a plurality of parties sufficient to transform the Soviet Union into a democratic society? And how will the CPSU adapt itself to the new situation?

Goals of the New Political Forces. One of the main obstacles to answering these questions is that it is now

84

almost impossible to speak of the Soviet Union as an entity. How long will the Soviet empire, of which one part—Lithuania—has already declared its independence, continue to exist? Similarly, the chances of the political opposition in the Soviet Union are difficult to assess, mainly because goals vary in different parts of the USSR.

In the Baltic republics, virtually all of the movements that represent the native populations want not only economic but also political independence from the rest of the Soviet Union. At the beginning of 1990, the popular fronts seemed to be the most powerful forces in these republics.[1] Unofficial movements representing the nonnative population in the area, which favor the Baltic republics' remaining within the USSR, have only insignificant influence.

In other parts of the Soviet Union, the drive for independence is also gaining strength. All in all, the goal of independence (or, at least, sovereignty) clearly gives political organizations in the non-Russian republics a base for consolidating opposition to the CPSU, which is associated with the idea of preserving the Soviet empire.

In the RSFSR, there is less certainty about the chances of new political movements' being able to consolidate their positions. During the first few months of 1990, at least three new political forces have demonstrated that they wield considerable influence in the RSFSR. They are the Interregional Group of Deputies, the Democratic Platform, and those soviets where, as in Moscow and Leningrad, democratic and non–Communist Party candidates have won majorities. At the same time, small—but politically weak—parties have been appearing (mostly in Moscow) virtually every day. These newly created parties range from liberal and Christian democrat to monarchist.

The Interregional Group of Deputies was able to draw tens of thousands of people to demonstrations in Moscow in February 1990, demanding that the CPSU relinquish its monopoly on power.[2] Some of its leaders—Yurii Afanas'ev, Gavriil Popov, and Boris Yeltsin—are among the most popular public figures in the country and have advanced the most radical proposals for democratizing the USSR; they have also sharply criticized the past and present Soviet leadership. In general, however, the difficulties encountered in reaching agreement and achieving any real consolidation have still weakened the chances of the Interregional Group's evolving into a unified opposition to the CPSU. Instead, the group is still essentially a conglomeration of powerful individuals rather than a united, influential political force capable of leading the country.

Among Moscow democrats, it would appear that occasionally the immediate goal of achieving personal power takes precedence over thought for the future of the country. Certainly, a number of leading public figures in Moscow have leveled such accusations against some of their colleagues. The economist Nikolai Shmelev, for example, has accused Gavriil Popov of publicly advocating the introduction of universal rationing in the USSR to curry favor among the masses, who erroneously regard rationing as an expression of social justice.[3] Shmelev argued that as an economist Popov should know that rationing would lead to abuses by officials distributing ration coupons rather than to any improvement in people's living standards. It is difficult to judge whether Shmelev's accusations are justified, but such accusations are serious and must be carefully considered.

Another somewhat disturbing phenomenon that has been observed in the political behavior of some democrats is a tendency to be intolerant toward those with differing views. Larisa Piyasheva, an economics commentator, revealed in *Izvestia* that she had been peremptorily dropped from the lists of candidates of the "Democratic Russia" bloc for seats in the RSFSR Congress of People's Deputies for daring to criticize statements by Il'ya Zaslavsky, who is a leader of the Interregional Group.[4] Many of the mistakes that democratic political figures make can probably be attributed to a lack of experience in implementing responsible political tasks. In addition, the political tradition of the

CPSU, characterized as it is by intolerance of dissent, has inevitably affected the CPSU's opponents.

If, however, the faults in the political strategy of Moscow democrats are set aside, it must be recognized that their main object is potentially the best existing political system for the Soviet Union—Western-style democracy. One of the most profound analyses of the proposed system has been provided by Andranik Migranyan, a philosopher and one of the most effective political theoreticians in Moscow. He expresses the hope that a civil society, as described in the writings of John Stuart Mill, John Locke, Adam Ferguson, and Alexis de Tocqueville, will eventually evolve in the Soviet Union. Among Migranyan's proposals to achieve this goal is the granting of "free self-organization in the economic, social, ethnic, cultural, and religious spheres." Political pluralism, according to Migranyan, should be combined with the legalization of private property and with the rule of law.[5]

Another political force that has quickly gained considerable influence in Moscow is the Democratic Platform of nonconformist Communists.[6] Commenting on the possibility of the Democratic Platform's causing a split within the CPSU, Moscow city party leader Yurii Prokof'ev argued that such a split would occur between radical reformist Communists, led by the Democratic Platform, and centrists, among whom Mikhail Gorbachev is currently the most powerful figure.[7] The conservatives—such as Egor Ligachev—have no significant support among the population, Prokof'ev said.

Prokof'ev is correct in assuming that if the split takes place at the Twenty-eighth Party Congress both parties will have a right to property that has hitherto belonged to the CPSU. The Democratic Platform will thereby immediately gain access to part of the party's finances, the press, buildings, and so forth, which will give the Democratic Platform a material base that other political groupings in the country currently lack. In this way, a split would give birth to at least two major political parties in the center, neither of which would have any great advantage over the other in its practical ability to exercise power. It remains to be seen how realistic the social democratic program of the nonconformist Communists will be. It is unclear how in so economically destabilized a country as the Soviet Union is today a relatively high living standard can be combined with firm social guarantees for the population as a whole.

The local government elections in the RSFSR, Belorussia, and Ukraine have created another new center of power—the soviets. As was true in the Baltic republics, these elections were marked by notable victories of democratic candidates from informal groups that advocate a multiparty system and a market economy. In such places as Leningrad and Moscow, for example, such candidates won majorities in the city soviets, which immediately began testing their actual access to power.

The Response of the CPSU. The leadership of the CPSU has been slow to react to the emergence of a multiparty system, which even some top party officials will admit. Yurii Prokof'ev, for example, has argued that political pluralism had been developing rapidly ever since the Nineteenth Party Conference, but that the leadership failed to react expeditiously.[8]

The first open acknowledgment of the changing role of the CPSU was made by the leadership at the Central Committee plenum held in February 1990. The plenum approved a draft platform of the CPSU Central Committee to be adopted at the Twenty-eighth Party Congress in July.[9] The platform expressed the party's readiness to relinquish its constitutionally guaranteed monopoly on power and to compete with other political organizations for influence in society. It nevertheless demonstrated that the party still hoped to remain the leading political force and a rallying point for the people in implementing democratization and reforms. Speaking after the plenum, one party official expressed the hope that all parties legalized in the Soviet Union would "stand on Socialist positions."[10]

The February plenum recommended that Article 6 of the USSR Constitution, which prescribed the leading role of the CPSU, be abolished—a recommendation that was followed by the USSR Congress of People's Deputies in March. The long-awaited law legalizing political parties in the USSR has not yet been adopted, however.

The reaction to these measures in many segments of Soviet society has tended to be negative. Even some party officials, among them Prokof'ev, have criticized the Central Committee platform for not looking ahead and for failing to define how the CPSU would operate within the framework of a legalized multiparty system. Representatives of the Democratic Platform have criticized the platform for refusing to consider a situation in which the CPSU, as is true of the East European Communist parties, might cease to be the most influential political force.[11]

Outspoken commentators have also criticized the leadership for failing to push through the law on political parties. In a penetrating analysis of the political situation in the USSR at the beginning of 1990, Liliya Shevtsova, a staff member of the USSR Academy of Sciences Institute of the Economics of the World Socialist System, argued that if the CPSU leadership persisted in underestimating the opposition, it could only lead the party to political ruin.[12] She proposed a law on political organizations that would legalize any party, including anti-Socialist ones. Only those groups that pursue racist or misanthropic aims should be outlawed, she argued.

Although representatives of the Democratic Platform believe that the CPSU has no chance of retaining the political leadership, Shevtsova does not exclude such a possibility. She considers that, in contrast to the Communist parties in Eastern Europe, the CPSU has one advantage—the absence in the Soviet Union of a united opposition. If, as things stand, the CPSU were to take the initiative, legalize political groups, factions among the deputies, popular fronts, and strike committees, and give them legal access to decision making by starting round-table talks with them on the East European pattern, the CPSU might have a chance of retaining the political leadership at least for a while. The weak point in Shevtsova's otherwise logical argument seems to be that she is projecting onto the whole of the country a situation that may pertain in the center of the USSR, but is completely ignoring those Union republics where the Communist Party has already lost the initiative to a united opposition.

These comments might suggest that at the beginning of 1990 the CPSU had ceased to devise any sort of policy to meet the challenge of the emerging multiparty system and was simply reacting belatedly to an uncontrollable process. This seems, however, not to be the case, for the CPSU apparently had a strategy of sorts for handling the newly emerging political forces—at least those in the center. This strategy is reflected in the reaction of the central media to the creation of new parties.

Many political groups that announced their arrival on the scene in Moscow as political parties in opposition to the CPSU at the beginning of 1990 have received quite extensive and sympathetic coverage on the *Vremya* television news program, which at that time was still strictly controlled by the Soviet authorities. In fact, the television coverage often portrayed newly established political groupings in a more influential capacity than they deserve.[13]

In discussing the reason for this approach, philosopher Igor Klyamkin may well be correct in surmising that the party leadership is seeking to splinter the opposition to retain its own position as the strongest single political force.[14] The more small, politically weak parties that are created, he argues, the better it is for the CPSU. The main threat to the CPSU is the Democratic Platform of nonconformist Communists, because it can cause a split in the ranks of the CPSU itself. In contrast to other newly created political groups in Moscow, the Democratic Platform has been strongly criticized in the party media and in a special statement by the CPSU Central Committee.[15] It seems that the CPSU leadership would be only too happy if supporters of the Democratic Platform were to establish their own social democratic party and quit the CPSU before the Twenty-eighth Party Congress, thereby obviating any need for power sharing or dividing party property. (The latter, as the situation in Lithuania demonstrates, can be a very painful process for both sides.) Calls made by top party officials, including Egor Ligachev, in April 1990, for a purge of "revisionists" from the ranks of the CPSU seem specifically designed to push nonconformist Communists into setting up their own party before the CPSU congress.[16]

It remains unclear how effective this strategy of the CPSU toward new political groupings will be, even in the short term. It may enable the CPSU to remain the most influential political force at the center for a time (the CPSU still holds a lot of the country's property and its officials still occupy important positions, especially in Russian provinces), but it is unlikely to do so for long now that the party has already lost the initiative to the opposition in some parts of the country.

Gorbachev's Role. Another important component in the likely development of the political situation in the USSR is the policy of Gorbachev himself, who is attempting to create a strong power base outside the CPSU. Is Gorbachev, who has so skillfully placed himself in the political center, intending to direct the USSR toward a civil society, as the new leaderships in East European countries have done? The answer to this question is not clear, because Gorbachev's political line is marked by inconsistencies, and his decisions often combine both democratic and strongly authoritarian elements.

Two recent developments—the creation of an executive presidency that Gorbachev has assumed as well as the membership of Gorbachev's Presidential Council—are cases in point. Commenting on the swearing in of Gorbachev as the first president of the USSR, people's deputy

Il'ya Zaslavsky said that Gorbachev would now "strengthen his personal power, which is bad, and start to break up the power of the CPSU, which is good."[17] Indeed, the law on the presidency shifts the base of power from the Communist Party to the state, limits the term of a leader in office, and ensures the election of the president by nationwide popular vote after the initial five-year term. At the same time, the law is encumbered with restrictions and contradictions that undercut its democratizing potential. It gives the president very broad powers, postpones the popular election of a president for five years, and provides none of the checks on executive power typical of Western democracies. The law clearly weakens the opportunities for a decentralization of power.

Moreover, Gorbachev has already demonstrated his capacity for using his broad presidential powers in violation of existing Soviet laws. The presidential decree of April 20, 1990, depriving the Moscow city council of regulating the conduct of demonstrations in the center of the Soviet capital, is a good illustration. (Gorbachev's decree was issued immediately upon the election of radical Gavriil Popov as Moscow's mayor.) According to the decree of the Presidium of the USSR Supreme Soviet on "The Ways Street Meetings and Demonstrations Should Be Held in the USSR," city soviets enjoy all the rights over governing public gatherings. Therefore, in issuing his decree, Gorbachev had obviously overstepped his powers, because as a president he can issue decrees, "based on Soviet laws and the Constitution." His decree limiting the right of the Moscow city soviet is issued, however, to change a law.

The composition of the Presidential Council, which was set up by Gorbachev's decree on March 24, 1990, again shows the Soviet leader's attempt to find a compromise between democrats and conservatives. Indeed, apart from the Politburo and CPSU Central Committee members, the council includes active spokesmen for both conservative and liberal groups of Soviet society, who do not occupy high official posts within the party apparatus. On the one hand, the council includes liberals—radical economist, academician Stanislav Shatalin, Vice President of the USSR Academy of Sciences Yurii Osipyan, and Kirghiz writer Chingiz Aitmatov. On the other hand, spokesmen for conservative and Russian nationalist groups (a leader in the United Front of Workers of Russia Veniamin Yarin and writer Valentin Rasputin) are also present in the council.[18]

The inclusion of Yarin in the council, immediately following the overwhelming defeat of candidates of the anti-reformist United Front of Workers of Russia in the RSFSR parliamentary elections, seems surprising. There are signs, however, that the conservative policies advocated by the United Front, especially in the economic sphere, have an influence on Gorbachev and his Presidential Council. Thus, on April 23, 1990, the council announced the further postponement of economic reforms.[19] Two days later, during his visit to the Ural city of Sverdlovsk, Gorbachev stressed that the USSR would not follow the Polish example of "shock-therapy," involving sudden, steep price rises and increased unemployment. Poland's radical economic reforms have been sharply criticized by the United Front. It seems to be more than a coincidence that Veniamin Yarin accompanied Gorbachev on his Urals trip.[20]

In sum, the emergence of a multiparty system in the USSR, with various political groups pursuing different—and at times opposing—goals, is coinciding with a period during which the central authorities are being inconsistent in their implementation of democratic reforms, and a legal basis for democratic changes already de facto achieved is not yet formed. Representatives of the new movements are often politically inexperienced, and the CPSU is facing a serious crisis that may well result in a split in its ranks, which makes the political situation highly unpredictable. As things stand, it is more likely that outbreaks of popular discontent will occur than that there will be a gradual transformation of the country into a democratic, multiparty state.

Appendix

Major Sociopolitical Movements in the USSR Other Than the CPSU

Existing sociopolitical movements embrace virtually every social, ethnic, and age group in Soviet society.[1] (A few of these movements—those of the Crimean Tatars and the Ukrainian Catholics, for example—appeared long before Mikhail Gorbachev launched his reforms.) The movements vary greatly in their aims, their influence among the population, and the numbers of their members and supporters. Although some of them are described by their organizers as parties, they are clearly not more important or influential than those that avoid the word "party" in their titles.

Popular Fronts

National Popular Fronts

Popular fronts now exist in all the Union republics and in the majority of autonomous republics and oblasts. Beginning with the promotion of all forms of national consciousness and national dignity, some of them have gradually evolved toward advocating political independence. The program documents of the popular fronts in the Baltic republics have served as models for the programs of popular fronts in other areas of the USSR.

Popular Fronts in the RSFSR

As of early 1990, an estimated 140 popular fronts have been established in cities and regions of the RSFSR, including Moscow, Leningrad, Yaroslavl, Tomsk, Stavropol, Chelyabinsk, Krasnoyarsk, Sverdlovsk (under the name Civic Forum), Tol'yatti, and Gorky. Members of the fronts are "Westerners" or "left-populists" in their outlook, and the groups with the largest memberships are those in Leningrad and Moscow. The Leningrad Popular Front, which is estimated to have 1 million supporters, won a sweeping victory in the elections to city and raion soviets in March 1990. There is also the Russian Popular Front, which considers the Bolshevik Revolution to have been a tragedy and flies the flag of St. Andrew at its demonstrations. It includes not only people who advocate democratic reforms but also some who are ideologically close to the extreme Russian nationalist organization *Pamyat'*.

Minority Movements

These movements include the associations of Crimean Tatars and Volga Germans, which were formed to promote the Tatars' return to the Crimea and the reestablishment of German autonomy on the Volga. Jewish groups as well as many ethnic solidarity groups have been established.

"Internationalist" Movements

These movements emerged in response to the surge of ethnic assertiveness in the Baltic area. They include various Interfront and Intermovement organizations in the Baltic republics, Moldavia, Tadzhikistan, and other areas. The United Council of Work Collectives in Estonia also belongs to this category. These groups opposed the independence movements of the non-Russian nationalities and have close links with conservative, including neo-Stalinist, circles in the RSFSR.

Russian Nationalist Groups

The best known of these are the various *Pamyat'* societies and similar "patriotic" organizations in Moscow, Leningrad, Siberia, and other parts of the RSFSR. Many of them are affiliated with the United Council of Russia, which was formed with the assistance of conservative party officials in 1989. Although these nationalists range from monarchists to neo-Stalinists, they are united in their hostility to the West and to non-Russian nationalism. Some of them support the theory of a "Judeo-Masonic conspiracy" against the Russian people.

On the eve of the parliamentary elections in the RSFSR, Moscow activists of a democratic orientation for the first time expressed concern that only conservative and chauvinistic forces had thus far been raising specifically Russian issues. To rectify the situation, Moscow democrats set up *Grazhdanskoe deistvie* (Civil Action), a group that is specifically intended to find a democratic solution to Russian problems.[2]

Party Clubs

In January 1990, 162 radical independent party clubs from 102 cities in 13 Union republics held a conference in Moscow to establish the Democratic Platform, which advocates a split within the CPSU and the creation of a social democratic party. The inaugural congress of the RSFSR Social Democratic Party was held in May 1990.

In April 1990, orthodox Communists formed the Marxist Platform, which is a group whose program contrasts with that of the Democratic Platform. The Marxist Platform has denounced the extension of private ownership to the means of production and calls for a return to "classic Marxism."[3]

Parliamentary Groups

The first parliamentary group, or faction, was set up by the Baltic deputies in the USSR Congress of People's Deputies. Currently, the most active parliamentary group at the all-Union level is the Interregional Group of Deputies. Democratic members of the newly elected RSFSR Congress of People's Deputies have set up their own "Democratic Russia" parliamentary bloc.[4]

There are also the conservative parliamentary groups *Rossiya* and *Soyuz*, which are dedicated to the preservation of "the integrity of the Soviet state," and the Union of Agrarian Workers, which is led by collective farm chairmen and state farm directors.

Independent Workers' Movements

These include the strike committees that demonstrated their ability to make and implement decisions during the miners' strikes in the summer of 1989. In addition, independent trade unions have been formed—initially in the Baltic republics and later elsewhere. In 1989 conservative party officials and representatives of elite workers established the United Fronts of Workers, which proclaimed as their aim the defense of workers' rights that were ignored or violated in the course of *perestroika*. It seems, however, that these fronts find little support among the majority of the working class.

Anti-Stalinist Groups

The best known of these is the Memorial society, which was first set up in Moscow in 1988 with the aim of collecting material on victims of Stalin's purges. Since then, branches of Memorial have been established in virtually all areas of the USSR. Its members have broadened their activities to include the collection of information about terror under Lenin.

Ecological and Cultural Movements

Ecological groups exist in virtually every part of the USSR. In Kazakhstan, Uzbekistan, and the Turkmen Republic, for instance, ecological movements are campaigning to save the areas around the Aral Sea and Lake Balkhash. There is also a thriving antinuclear movement in Kazakhstan. The largest of the ecological groups is believed to be the Ukrainian *Zelenyi svit* (Green World). Efforts are said to be under way to unite approximately 300 ecological clubs in a green party.

Cultural movements set up in 1986 and 1987 for the purpose of preserving historical monuments in Leningrad and other Russian cities were the first informal public groups to raise political questions openly after *perestroika* was introduced. Similar groups exist in other Union republics.

Religious Groups

Groups have been formed in various parts of the Soviet Union (for example, "Church and *Perestroika*" in Moscow) to defend religious rights and to encourage believers to participate in the political life of the country. One of the largest movements is that of the Ukrainian Catholics for the legalization of their Church. The movement existed before Gorbachev initiated *perestroika*, but only in the past year has it been able to emerge from the underground. Membership has risen perceptibly since.

Military Groups

There are several unofficial military groups, the best known of which is *Shchit* (Shield), a trade union for servicemen. There are also groups of Afghan veterans, campaigning for what they consider social justice, that maintain close contacts with *Pamyat'* societies. In early 1990 a Sakharov Union of Democratic Afghan War Veterans was established. Its goal is "the defense of democratic activities," which includes providing bodyguards for members of anti-Stalinist Memorial societies and other democratic organizations that come under attack from *Pamyat'*.[5]

Fledgling Parties

These first made their appearance in the Baltic republics. In other Union republics, independence movements that press their demands further than the popular fronts tend to call themselves parties (the National Independence Party of Georgia and the Party of National Self-Determination of Armenia, for example).

In Moscow, the first group to call itself a political party was the Democratic Union, which was set up in 1988 to fight against the existing Soviet system. In 1990 almost daily some group announces the formation of a new political party in the capital. The most recent examples are the Party of Liberal Democrats (Kadets), who advocate the de-ideologization of society, and the Party of Christian Democrats, who want to combine Western-style parliamentary democracy with greater participation of the Church in state affairs.[6] These new parties are as yet relatively small and possess little political clout.

Notes

Chapter 1

1. Stephen F. Cohen and Katerina van den Heuvel, *Voices of Glasnost': Interviews with Gorbachev's Reformers* (New York: W. W. Norton and Company, 1989), 39.

2. Fedor Burlatsky, "Pervyi, no vazhnyi shag," *Literaturnaya gazeta*, June 14, 1989.

3. *Pravda*, March 30, 1987.

4. A. D. Stepansky, *Istoriya obshchestvennykh organizatsii dorevolyutsionnoi Rossii* (Moscow: Nauka, 1979), 67.

5. *Pamyat': Istoricheskii sbornik*, vol. 4 (Moscow 1979–Paris 1981), 128–129.

6. A. P. Pinkevich, "Vserossiiskaya kraevedcheskaya konferentsiya," *Nauchnyi rabotnik*, no. 1 (1928): 9–11.

7. *Nauchnyi rabotnik*, no. 11–12 (1930): 69.

8. *Pamyat'*, vol. 1 (Moscow 1976–New York 1978): 232–268; vol. 3 (Moscow 1978–1980): 539–557; vol. 5 (Moscow 1981–Paris 1982): 226–227.

9. Moshe Levin, *The Gorbachev Phenomenon: A Historical Interpretation* (London: Radius, 1988), 80.

10. Valentina Levicheva, "Neformal'naya gruppa: ishchem sebya," *Smena*, no. 12 (1987): 5.

11. *Komsomol'skaya pravda*, October 10, 1987; *Sotsialisticheskaya industriya*, March 25, 1987.

12. S. I. Plaksii, *Politicheskoe samoobrazovanie*, no. 7 (1988): 84.

13. *Pravda*, March 30, 1987.

14. *Sotsialisticheskaya industriya*, March 25, 1987; *Radio Moscow*-1 (0915), January 4, 1987 (talk with the writer Mikhail Antonov on problems of the upbringing of Soviet youth).

15. L. L. Lisyutkina and A. D. Khlopin, *Neformal'nye gruppy v SSSR: Potentsial perestroiki obshchestvennykh otnoshenii*. The report was not published in the Soviet press. Both Lisyutkina and Khlopin are specialists on social movements in the West. They were asked to apply their methodology to similar phenomena in the Soviet Union.

16. The draft program of the Moscow Popular Front, Chapter 1, "The Main Principles of the Front's Activities."

Chapter 2

1. On February 2, 1988, *Novosti* press agency issued a commentary, saying that there were more than 30,000 informal groups. See also, O. Shenin, "Za steklyannoi stenoi," *Pravda*, February 5, 1988, p. 3, giving the same figure.

2. Article by Roy Medvedev in *La Repubblica*, October 11–12, 1987, p. 11.

3. On December 7, 1989, the Lithuanian Supreme Soviet voted to eliminate the clause on the leading role of the Communist Party from the Lithuanian Constitution. The new article of the Lithuanian Constitution, which replaced one on the party's leading role, legalized a multiparty system in the republic (*TASS*, December 8, 1989).

4. *Pravda*, "Demokratiya ne terpit demagogii," February 10, 1989.

5. A plenum of the CPSU Central Committee held in February 1990 recommended the abolition of Article 6 of the Constitution. On March 13, 1990, the USSR Congress of People's Deputies confirmed the abolition (*Pravda*, March 14, 1990).

6. A. Ignatov, "Shagat' navstrechu," *Komsomol'skaya pravda*, October 10, 1986.

7. Pavel Ermishev, "'Bolevye tochki' molodezhnoi estrady," *Smena*, no. 4 (1985): 6–7. For the details on music ensembles, see AS 5519 and an accompanying commentary.

8. *Pravda*, March 30, 1987; Aleksandr Radov, "Deti Detochkina," *Komsomol'skaya pravda*, October 17, 1986.

9. *Komsomol'skoe znamya*, December 6, 1986; *Komsomol'skaya pravda*, August 23, 1985. See also, Vera Tolz, "Controversy in Soviet Press over Unofficial Youth Groups," RL 99/87, March 11, 1987.

10. One of the most active has been the Leningrad literary group "Klub 81," which continued its activities after Gorbachev came to power. It united in its ranks the most famous Leningrad literary figures.

11. RL 147/82, Boris Groys, "Journals of the 'Second Culture' in Leningrad," March 31, 1982. *Komsomol'skoe znamya*, January 18, 1987.

12. *Komsomol'skaya pravda*, October 17, 1986.

13. Ibid., January 8, 1986.

14. *Izvestia*, June 3, 1987; *Ogonek*, no. 20 (1987); *Literaturnaya gazeta*, May 20, 1987.

15. Julia Wishnevsky, "El'tsyn Meets with Members of *'Pamyat'*," RL 191/87, May 19, 1987, and Julia Wishnevsky, "The Emergence of *'Pamyat'* and *'Otechestvo'*," RL 342/87, August 26, 1987.

16. Wishnevsky, "El'tsyn Meets with Members of *'Pamyat'*."

17. This document is kept in Radio Liberty Archives of Samizdat.

18. *Moscow News*, no. 32 (1988); *Literaturnaya gazeta*, no. 32 (1988); *Leningradskaya pravda*, August 12 and 18, 1988; *Izvestia*, August 14, 1988.

19. *Vestnik Akademii Nauk SSSR*, no. 10 (1989): 93–94.

20. Dawn Mann and Julia Wishnevsky, "Composition of Congress of People's Deputies," *Report on the USSR*, no. 18 (1989): 1–6; and Julia Wishnevsky, "Patriots Urge Annulment of RSFSR Elections," *Report on the USSR* 2, no. 14 (1990): 18–21.

21. *Izvestia*, March 27, 1987 and April 9, 1987; *Literaturnaya gazeta*, March 25, 1987 and May 20, 1987. In contrast, the conservative *Leningradskaya pravda* of March 21, 1987, negatively assessed the activities of the Leningrad informal groups.

22. *Stroitel'naya gazeta*, April 24, 1987.

23. *Izvestia*, March 27, 1987.

24. Bohdan Nahaylo, "Informal Ukrainian Culturological Club Helps to Break New Ground for Glasnost'," RL 57/88, Feb-

ruary 8, 1988; Kathleen Mihalisko, "A Profile of Informal Patriotic Youth Groups in Belorussia," RL 318/88, July 14, 1988. On the "Ukrainian Association of Independent Creative Intelligentsia," see *Russkaya mysl'*, September 9, 1988.

25. Bohdan Nahaylo, "Independent Groups in Ukraine under Attack," RL 417/88, September 12, 1988; Kathleen Mihalisko, "Belorussian Activists Are Charged with Violating Law on Unauthorized Assemblies," RL 418/88, September 14, 1988. In October 1988, a group of Belorussian officials rudely attacked members of the "Talaka Society"; see *Sovetskaya Belorussiya*, October 22, 1988, and *Znamya yunosti*, October 23, 1988.

26. Vera Tolz, "Informal Groups in Soviet Political Life," *Washington Quarterly* 11, no. 2 (Spring 1988): 137–155.

27. *Moscow News*, no. 19 (1988), and *Sovetskaya kul'tura*, April 28, 1988.

28. See Boris Kurashvili on the popular front in *Moscow News*, March 6, 1988 (a brief note), in *Sovetskaya molodezh'*, April 27, 1988, and in *Sovetskaya Kirgizia*, May 11, 1988. Zaslavskaya endorsed the idea of the front at a press conference in Moscow on May 23 (*Reuters*, May 23, 1988).

29. See, for instance, an interview with members of the Leningrad *Obnovlenie* club in *Vechernii Leningrad*, October 6, 1988. One example of the controversy concerning what attitude the informal groups should take toward the current policies of the Soviet leadership is the polemic between Leningrad unofficial activists published in the Paris-based émigré journal *Sintaksis*, no. 21 (1988): 67–81.

30. *Molodezh' Estonii, Sovetskaya Estoniya*, November 5, 1988; *Sovetskaya Latvia*, October 18, 1988; *Komsomol'skaya pravda* (Lithuania), October 26, 1988.

31. In June 1988, representatives of unofficial groups from the Union republics—the Party of National Independence of Estonia, the Lithuanian Freedom League, the Ukrainian Helsinki Federation, and the Party of National Self-Determination of Armenia—set up a "Coordinating Committee of the Patriotic Movements of the Peoples of the USSR" (see Bohdan Nahaylo, "Representatives of Non-Russian National Movements Establish Coordinating Committee," RL 283/88, June 22, 1988).

32. *Sovetskaya molodezh'*, October 11, 1988; *Sovetskaya Latvia*, October 18, 1988; *Sovetskaya Estoniya* and *Molodezh' Estonii*, October 5, 1988.

33. See Vera Tolz, "The USSR This Week," *Report on the USSR*, no. 10 (1989): 50.

34. This was reported on *RFE Estonian Service*, December 15, 1989.

35. On the negative attitude of the Ukrainian authorities toward the plans for the creation of the "Popular Front for the Support of *Perestroika*" in Kiev, see *Robitnycha hazeta*, October 4, 1988. On the negative attitude of conservative officials toward informal groups in Belorussia, see an article by Belorussian writers Ales' Adamovich and Vasyl Bykov in *Moscow News*, no. 45 (1988); see also, *Sovetskaya Belorussiya*, October 27, 1988, on the attack by hard-liners.

36. For the details of the economic blockade of Armenia and the Nagorno-Karabakh Autonomous Oblast organized by the Azerbaijani Popular Front, see, for instance, Vera Tolz, "The USSR This Week," *Report on the USSR*, no. 39 (1989): 25–26; no. 40 (1989): 26; no. 41 (1989): 34–35; and no. 42 (1989): 26–27.

37. The reinstitution of the use of Latin script was approved by the Moldavian Supreme Soviet at a four-day session ending on September 1, 1989; see Vladimir Socor, "Moldavian Proclaimed Official Language in the Moldavian SSR," *Report on the USSR*, no. 38 (1989): 13–15.

38. Vera Tolz and Melanie Newton, "The USSR This Week," *Report on the USSR*, no. 44 (1989): 33.

39. See, for example, a report in *Izvestia*, October 27, 1989, revealing that the Soviet government decided to halt construction of a nuclear plant in the Crimea in response to pressure from the public.

40. "Nevada," which was formed in February 1989, sponsored a demonstration in Kazakhstan on October 21, 1989, by thousands of people who demanded an end to nuclear tests at Semipalatinsk (*Reuters*, October 21, 1989). As a result of the public pressure, the Kazakh Supreme Soviet and the republican party appealed to the central authorities to end nuclear tests in the area (*TASS*, November 14, 1989).

41. *APN*, February 14, 1990.

42. Irina Snezhkova in *Obshchestvennye nauki*, no. 6 (1989): 116.

43. *Moscow News*, no. 40 (1988), printed a gloomy picture of the Moscow Popular Front as torn by internal strife. The article

was written by a leading member of the unofficial political movement in Moscow, Gleb Pavlovsky.

44. Snezhkova, *Obshchestvennye nauki*, 118. See also Mark Lyubomudrov in *Literaturnaya Rossiya*, no. 8 (1988).

45. *Sovetskaya molodezh'*, January 26, 1989.

46. Snezhkova, *Obshchestvennye nauki*, 119.

47. *Sovetskaya kul'tura*, March 17, 1990, an interview with Moscow city party boss Yurii Prokof'ev.

48. On Moscow's "Memorial," see *Ogonek*, nos. 41 and 47 (1988); *Neva*, no. 10 (1988): 152–162; *Znamya yunosti*, February 10, 1989. On branches of the Memorial in other parts of the USSR, see, for instance, *Komsomol'skaya pravda*, March 3, 1989 on the branch of the Memorial set up in the Karaganda Oblast and the Odessa periodical *Znamya kommunisma*, March 5, 1989 on the Odessa branch of the society.

Chapter 3

1. *Ogonek*, no. 36 (1987); *Moscow News*, no. 37 (1987).

2. *Guardian*, September 12, 1987.

3. See *Vesti iz SSSR/USSR News Brief*, no. 16–5 (1982).

4. See Julia Wishnevsky, "More Details Emerge about 'Socialists' Arrested in the USSR Earlier This Year," RL 341/82, August 23, 1982, and idem, "*Samizdat* Symposium *Sotsialist*-82 Reaches the West," RL 41/83, January 20, 1983.

5. *Bulletin of Radio Liberty Samizdat Department*, AS 6015.

6. AS 6127 and 6132.

7. *Sovetskaya bibliografiya*, no. 2 (1989): 26.

8. Saulius Girnius, "Unofficial Groups in the Baltic Republics and Access to the Mass Media," in Baltic Area Situation Report/4, *Radio Free Europe Research*, April 21, 1989. See also, *Sovetskaya bibliografiya*, no. 5 (1989): 13–18.

9. *Sovetskaya bibliografiya*, no. 2 (1989).

10. *Moscow News*, no. 47 (1989).

11. It is possible that *Vechernii Leningrad* will soon change its political orientation because in April 1990 it became the organ of the newly elected Leningrad City Council, where representatives of the Leningrad Popular Front constitute a majority.

12. For the text of the draft press law, see *Izvestia*, December 4, 1989.

13. *Knizhnoe obozrenie*, no. 15 (1990).

14. *Vestnik Akademii Nauk*, no. 10 (1989): 88.

15. *Moscow News*, no. 34, August 20, 1989.

16. *Literaturnaya gazeta*, April 11, 1990.

17. See Saulius Girnius, "Sajudis Candidates Sweep Elections in Lithuania," *Report on the USSR*, no. 15 (1989): 29–30.

18. This was emphasized by Chairman of the Moscow Oblast Executive Committee Nikolai Shalyapin in an interview with *TASS* on December 22, 1989.

19. In preparation for the first elections to the USSR Congress of People's Deputies, an independent association, "Elections 89," was set up in Leningrad. In Moscow, an association of voters was created whose city committee has been publishing an independent periodical, *Khronika*, since March 5, 1989.

20. "Po zamyslu neformalov," *Russkaya mysl'*, February 2, 1990.

21. For more information about the Vologda city association of voters, see *Sobesednik*, no. 49 (1989). The Sverdlovsk association is discussed in *Sovetskaya molodezh'*, January 26, 1990. For reports on such associations in other Siberian cities, see the unofficial *Pres byulleten'* of the Independent Siberian Information Agency, no. 38 (1989), and nos. 1 and 2 (1990).

22. See the report on the inaugural congress of the All-Union Association of Voters in the periodical of the Melitopol branch of the Popular Movement of Ukraine for *Perestroika (Rukh)*, *Probuzhdenie*, no. 11 (1989).

23. The principles of the Interregional Group of Deputies seem to have a strong influence on the electoral platforms of many candidates from informal groups, including the Khabarovsk Popular Front and the informal bloc of candidates called "Democratic Russia." The influence exercised by the Interregional Group seems to bother party officials, who are quoted on this matter in *Partiinaya zhizn'*, no. 2 (1990): 32.

24. *Russkaya mysl'*, September 29, 1989, p. 4.

25. Reported by the unofficial journal *Pozitsiya*, no. 4 (December 1989): 5 and 8.

26. *Sovetskaya molodezh'*, January 26, 1989.

27. *Russkaya mysl'*, February 2, 1990.

28. Ibid.

29. The call by the Democratic Union for a boycott of the elections was reported by *Tanjug*, January 17, 1990. For more about the anarcho-syndicalists, see *Russkaya mysl'*, February 2, 1990.

30. *Express Khronika*, no. 4 (1990) and *Leningradsky literator*, no. 2 (1990): 2.

31. *Sovetskaya molodezh'*, January 26, 1990, and *Ogonek*, no. 6 (1990).

32. For the text of the platform, see *Literaturnaya Rossiya*, December 29, 1989. See also, Paul Goble, "Platform of the Russian Patriotic Bloc," *Report on the USSR*, no. 2 (1990): 11–12.

33. The club *Rossiya* was set up in October 1989 (*Radio Moscow*-1, 2350, October 24, 1989).

34. This information was given to the author by spokesmen for informal groups in Leningrad.

35. *Sovetskaya Rossiya*, January 27, 1990.

36. *Sibirskaya gazeta*, January 15, 1990, quotes excerpts from Manannikov's platform, the full text of which appears in the *Pres byulleten'* of the Independent Siberian Information Agency, no. 36 (1989).

37. The Samizdat Staff of Radio Liberty has a copy of the full text of the election platform of the Khabarovsk Popular Front. The idea of setting up a Far Eastern Republic recently received support from a group of deputies from the Far East and Siberia (*Novosti*, February 14, 1990).

38. This leaflet is quoted in the *Pres byulleten'* of the Independent Siberian Information Agency, no. 38 (1989): 1.

39. Ibid., 2.

40. See *Russkaya mysl'*, February 2, 1990. The authorities also initially wanted to block the registration of Manannikov's candidacy for election (see *Sovetskaya Sibir'*, January 14, 1990). The *Pres byulleten'* of the Independent Siberian Information Agency (no. 2 [1990]: 6) also reports that the local electoral committee in Novosibirsk refused to register *samizdat* journalist Aleksei Kretinin as a candidate, alleging that the registration form had been filled out incorrectly.

41. *Izvestia*, January 2, 1990; *Sovetskaya Rossiya*, February 3 and 10, 1990; *Argumenty i fakty*, no. 1 (1990). Violations of the law in the nomination of party candidates for the elections were discussed in a telebridge between Moscow, Tashkent, and Kishinev broadcast by Soviet television on January 24, 1990. The

Pres byulleten' of the Independent Siberian Information Agency (no. 1 [1990]: 4) reports on violations of the RSFSR law on elections in the nomination of First Secretary of the Novosibirsk City Party Committee Anatolii Maslov at a local factory.

42. The *Pres byulleten'* of the Independent Siberian Information Agency (no. 38 [1989]: 4) reports on such a case in the Siberian city of Berdsk.

43. *Partiinaya zhizn'*, no. 2 (1990): 34, reports that the Khabarovsk Krai Party Committee proposed to local political groups that they draft a common electoral platform. Attempts by Leningrad party and government officials to use the Leningrad Popular Front for their own purposes in the preelection campaign are described in *Leningradskii literator*, no. 2 (1990). In Irkutsk, party officials and informal groups got together to create a joint election bloc; see the report by V. B. Pastukhov in *Vybory-90*, no. 4, p. 8. (*Vybory-90* is a newsletter published by the Center for Political and Legal Research and Information, which was set up by *Moscow News*.)

44. Saulius Girnius, "Results of Lithuanian Supreme Soviet Elections," *Report on the USSR* 2, no. 10 (1990): 2324.

45. *Russkaya mysl'*, February 2, 1990, and *Argumenty i fakty*, no. 7 (1990).

46. *Moscow News*, no. 12 (1990): 4.

47. *Radio Moscow*, April 9, 1990.

48. See Julia Wishnevsky, "Patriots Urge Annulment of RSFSR Elections," *Report on the USSR* 2, no. 14 (1990): 1821.

49. *Radio Kiev*, April 18, 1990.

50. The dismissal of the Leningrad TV chief was reported by *Reuters*, April 7, 1990. The dismissal was condemned in the Soviet press. See, for instance, *Nedelya*, no. 15 (1990). The pro-Lithuanian demonstration took place on April 8 (*Soviet Television*, "Vermya," April 8, 1990), and on April 10 *Sovetskaya Rossiya* criticized the Leningrad City Council for authorizing it.

Chapter 4

1. *Radio Moscow-2* (1430), February 26, 1987.
2. *Komsomol'skaya pravda*, October 10, 1989.
3. *Ogonek*, no. 5 (1987).
4. *Pravda*, March 30, 1987.

5. On the trust group see, for instance, Julia Wishnevsky, "The Trial of Olga Medvedekova," RL 130/84, March 27, 1984; *The USSR News Brief*, no. 24 (1986); *UPI*, February 15, 1987. On the Gursuf group, see *Komsomol'skaya pravda*, January 18, 1987.

6. *Reuters*, November 1, 1988.

7. On October 14, 1988, *Reuters* and *AFP* reported that several members of the "Democratic Union" were detained and fined for participating in an unauthorized demonstration in Moscow.

8. On October 27, 1988, *Sovetskaya kul'tura* published a letter by a group of jurists criticizing the decrees. The decrees, however, were approved by a session of the USSR Supreme Soviet on October 28, 1988 (*TASS*, October 28, 1988).

9. For the sharp criticism of the party's past and current policies, see, for example, Igor Klyamkin in *Novyi mir*, no. 2 (1989).

10. *TASS*, February 10, 1989. Chebrikov reiterated this position at a meeting of aviation workers in Moscow (*TASS*, June 27, 1989) and in an article in *Kommunist*, no. 8 (1989).

11. *Pravda*, July 21, 1989.

12. Gorbachev's speech was not published in the USSR; see Michael Dobbs, "Gorbachev Criticizes Irresponsible Editors," *Washington Post*, October 17, 1989; Bill Keller, "Gorbachev Waffles on Glasnost," *New York Times*, October 19, 1989; and David Remnick, "Gorbachev Seen to Take a Sharp Conservative Turn," *Washington Post*, October 19, 1989.

Chapter 5

1. *Komsomol'skaya pravda*, October 10, 1986.

2. Ibid.

3. *Literaturnaya gazeta*, May 20, 1987.

4. *Radio Moscow-1* (1500 and 1900), December 17, 1986.

5. See the chapter on the first officially sanctioned conference of unofficial groups.

6. See, for instance, Vladimir Lysenko, "Krizis partii i puti vykhoda iz nego," *Politika*, no. 1 (1990): 36; see also a commentary by Mikhail Poltoranin on the role of popular fronts, carried by the Novosti press agency on February 14, 1990.

7. A report on the Novosibirsk seminar appeared in *Par-*

tiinaya zhizn', no. 2 (1990): 31–36; a report on the Vitebsk seminar appeared in *Partiinaya zhizn'*, no. 3 (1990): 29–33.

8. Murmansky oblastnoi komitet KPSS. Dom politicheskogo prosveshcheniya. *Murmanskaya oblast: voprosy i otvety*, no. 7 (Murmansk: 1989).

9. Lisyutkina and Khlopin, *Neformal'nye gruppy v SSSR: potentsial perestroiki obshchestvennykh otnoshenii*. See chapter 1, n. 15, this volume.

10. Irina Snezhkova, "Natsionalnye aspekty programm neformal'nykh ob'edinenii," *Obshchestvennye nauki*, no. 6 (1989): 110–122.

11. *Partiinaya zhizn'*, no. 2 (1990): 36.

Chapter 6

1. *UPI*, May 7, *AP*, May 8, *Washington Post*, May 8, *UPI*, May 8, *AP*, May 9, 1988.

2. Martin Walker in *Guardian*, May 9, 1988, lists the main unofficial groups that participated in setting up the Democratic Union.

3. For the criticism of the seminar "Democracy and Humanism," see, for instance, *Sobesednik*, no. 44 (October 1987). Although the Group for the Establishment of Trust between East and West was for years regularly criticized in the Soviet press, in December 1987, members of the group were allowed to express their views on Soviet television (see Elizabeth Teague, "Moscow TV Airs Views of Independent Peace Group," RL 498/87, December 8, 1987).

4. *Reuters*, May 9, 1988.

5. *Reuters, UPI*, February 2, 1988. See Baltic Situation Report/2, *Radio Free Europe Research*, February 16, 1987, item 2.

6. See AS 5724 and RL 282/86, Vera Tolz, "Predecessors of the *Samizdat* Appeal 'To the Citizens of the Soviet Union,'" July 28, 1986.

7. *Ogonek*, no. 36 (1987), and *Moscow News*, no. 37 (1987).

8. Since April 1988, Soviet newspapers have carried a good many letters by readers who have proposed significant changes in the Soviet political system. See, for instance, *Sovetskaya kul'tura*, April 9 and 30, 1988; and *Pravda*, May 2 and 8, 1988.

9. *AP*, February 13, 1988; *USSR News Brief*, 1/2–41, 1988.

10. *Krasnaya zvezda*, December 10, 1987.

11. On May 10, 1988, *AFP* quoted Debryanskaya as having said that 70 people voted on May 9 on the union's aims, which included the introduction of political pluralism in the USSR, the establishment of free trade unions and a free press, and opposition to the KGB. In 1988–1989, branches of the Democratic Union were set up in many Soviet cities, with the most active in Leningrad and Novosibirsk. According to spokesmen of the Democratic Union, by the end of 1989, the organization had approximately 2,000 members.

12. *Moscow News*, no. 26, June 25, 1989.

13. On June 16, on the eve of the constituent congress of the Leningrad Popular Front, the Leningrad Komsomol newspaper *Smena* carried Sergei Andreev's declaration on the aims and structure of the front.

14. *Sovetskaya molodezh'*, June 22, 1989.

15. *Tartusky Kur'er*, no. 1 (June 1–15, 1989): 8. The issue also carried the rules of the Leningrad Popular Front and other materials on the situation in Leningrad.

16. *Leningradskaya pravda*, June 8 and 14, 1989.

17. *Sotsialisticheskaya industriya*, July 11, 1989.

18. *Tartusky Kur'er*, no. 1 (1989): 8.

19. *Reuters*, July 13, 1989.

20. *Trud*, June 24, 1989.

21. *TASS*, July 12, 1989.

22. "Vremya" TV news program, July 12, 1989.

23. For the text of Gidaspov's speech, see *Leningradskaya pravda*, November 22, 1989.

24. There were few places in the RSFSR where local councils supported the idea of holding experimental elections in factory-based electoral districts. Altogether 49 factory-based districts were involved in the experiment. Among these districts one was set up in Moscow's raion of Tushino. The main newspaper of this region, *Golos Tushina*, strongly supports the United Front of Workers and other extreme Russian nationalist organizations. The experimental elections seem not to show desirable results, however, because even there the candidates of the United Front of Workers were not supported by the voters. See Dawn Mann, "The RSFSR Elections: Factory-Based Constituencies," in *Report on the USSR* 2, no. 14 (1990): 16–18.

25. See the chapter on unofficial groups and elections.

26. *Sovetskaya Rossiya*, September 13, 1989.

27. *Central Television*, 1630, September 17, 1989.

28. See Vera Tolz, "Politics in Leningrad and the Creation of Two Popular Fronts," *Report on the USSR*, no. 29 (1989): 38–40. There are also several items on the Leningrad United Front of Workers in *Tartusky Kur'er*, no. 3 (1989), including one written by writer Mikhail Chulaki, who reveals that Yurii Solov'ev attended one of the sessions of the front's inaugural congress. It was at this session that changes in election law proposed by the front were discussed. On the relationship between the Leningrad United Front of Workers and the Leningrad party apparatus, see also *Sovetskaya kul'tura*, September 16, 1989.

29. *Leningrad Television*, May 11, 1989. See the reference to Pyzhov's election speech in Lev Karpinsky's article in *Moscow News*, no. 21 (1989).

30. On the defeat of Sverdlovsk party officials in the elections of Spring 1989, see *Pravda*, July 15, 1989.

31. *Baltimore Sun*, September 14, 1989.

32. According to *Leningradskaya pravda* (May 17, 1989), Pyzhov received only 0.67 percent of the vote.

33. Further evidence of the lack of support among representatives of the working class for the united fronts of workers could be found in Belorussia. Radio Liberty's Belorussian Service received a report that 208 workers (which is more than the number of delegates at the Sverdlovsk congress) had decided to create a Belorussian workers' union to counter efforts to create a united front of workers in the Belorussian capital of Minsk. The 208 workers suggested that it was the party apparatus that wanted to create the united front in the republic and that the purpose was to set workers against intellectuals.

34. On September 15, *TASS* quoted the Moldavian party leadership as saying that strikes by workers in the republic in protest against the law to make Moldavian the republic's state language had cost the Soviet economy "tens of millions of rubles." In Tadzhikistan, too, whence came some of the Russian-speaking workers who participated in the congress of the United Front of Workers of Russia, new laws were causing concern among the non-Tadzhik population. On September 16, *Izvestia* reported that 10,000 non-Tadzhik-speaking people left the capital, Dushanbe, during the first half of 1989. The newspaper attributed this emigration principally to the recent decision by the re-

public's Supreme Soviet to make Tadzhik the official language. The newspaper also claimed that people were afraid that events in the Baltic and Moldavia might repeat themselves in Tadzhikistan.

35. *Sovetskaya Rossiya*, September 14, 1989.

36. Regarding conservative Russian-nationalist cultural figures, see Julia Wishnevsky, "*Nash Sovremennik* Provides Focus for 'Opposition Party,'" *Report on the USSR*, no. 3 (1989): 1–6; idem, "Ligachev, 'Pamyat', and Conservative Writers," in ibid., no. 10 (1989): 12–15, and Douglas Smith, "Formation of New Russian Nationalist Group Announced," in ibid., no. 27 (1989): 5–8.

37. See Dawn Mann and Julia Wishnevsky, "Composition of Congress of People's Deputies," *Report on the USSR*, no. 18 (1989): 4.

38. Pastukhov's comments appeared on page 7 of *Vybory-90* – a special issue prepared by the Center for Political and Legal Research and Information attached to *Moscow News*.

39. *Ogonek*, no. 8 (1990): 5.

40. *Literaturnaya Rossiya*, no. 52 (1989): 2–3.

41. *Leningradskii literator*, January 10, 1990, p. 3.

42. This point has been made many times by Yurii Afanas'ev (see, for example, his speech on Soviet television on December 9, 1989).

43. As cited by Scott Shane in *Baltimore Sun*, March 21, 1990.

44. *Times* (London), March 6, 1990.

45. *Moskovskie novosti*, no. 9 (1990): 14.

46. See Elizabeth Teague, "Gorbachev Criticizes Leaders of Parliamentary Group," *Report on the USSR*, no. 43 (October 27, 1989): 2.

47. *Literaturnaya gazeta*, August 2, 1989, p. 2.

48. Ibid.; *TASS*, July 30, 1989; *Sotsialisticheskaya industriya*, August 1, 1989.

49. *Smena*, September 23, 1989.

50. *TASS*, July 30, 1989.

51. "Vremya," July 29, 1989.

52. *TASS*, July 30; *New York Times*, July 30, 1989; *Los Angeles Times*, July 31, 1989.

53. *TASS*, July 30, 1989; *Sotsialisticheskaya industriya*, August 1, 1989.

54. The activities of the Interregional Group yielded positive

results. Many independent voters' clubs were created in various regions of the USSR; see *Moscow News*, no. 49 (1989).

55. *Literaturnaya gazeta*, February 2, 1989, p. 2.

56. For the text of Afanas'ev's speech, see the periodical of the Estonian Popular Front, *Tartusky kur'er*, no. 5 (September 1–15, 1989).

57. For the text of the draft program see *Tartusky kur'er*, no. 5 (1989). See also *AP*, September 24, 1989.

58. The draft of the new Soviet Constitution, prepared by Sakharov, was published in *Komsomol'skaya pravda* (Lithuania), December 12, 1989.

59. *Radio Moscow*, August 4, 1989.

60. See Vera Tolz, "The Implications for *Glasnost'* of Gorbachev's Attack on Reformists," *Report on the USSR*, no. 43 (1989): 5–9.

61. Primakov's displeasure with the creation of the interregional groups was reported in *Literaturnaya gazeta*, August 2, 1989 and by Bill Keller in *New York Times*, July 30, 1989.

62. *Soviet Television*, August 7, 1989.

63. See, for instance, *Moscow News*, no. 32, which carried an attack on the Interregional Group by Veli Gusein ogly Mamedov, a deputy from Baku. A spokesman for the United Front of Workers of Russia, Anatolii Salutsky, attacked the Interregional Group in *Literaturnaya Rossiya*, no. 40 (1989).

64. *Russkaya mysl'*, September 29, 1989, p. 4.

65. Ibid., and Elizabeth Teague, "Moscow TV Airs Views of Independent Peace Group," 3.

66. Cited in *Russkaya mysl'*, September 29, 1989, p. 4.

67. Western agencies reported the call for the strike on December 2. A few days later, Yurii Chernichenko withdrew his signature under the appeal for the strike (*Izvestiya*, December 6, 1989).

68. *Reuters, AP*, December 14, 1989.

69. *AP*, December 15, 1989.

70. This was stated by Yurii Afanas'ev and other radical members of the Interregional Group in talks with Western correspondents and Radio Liberty.

71. See, for instance, Yurii Bandura in *Moscow News*, March 25, 1990, and Anatolii Latyshev in ibid., September 10, 1989.

72. Now in all the Baltic republics, there are Communist parties independent of the CPSU. In Lithuania and Estonia,

these parties are larger than those groups of Communists that continue to stress their loyalty to Moscow. (In Latvia, the independent Communist Party is smaller than the pro-Moscow one.)

73. The newly created Social Democratic parties have already gathered together to form the Social Democratic Association. The association held its inaugural congress in Tallinn on January 14, 1990, which was attended by delegates not only from the Baltics but also from various cities of the RSFSR, Uzbekistan, Belorussia, and Azerbaijan (*Literaturnaya gazeta*, January 17, 1990). On social democrats in Georgia, see *Molodezh' Gruzii*, November 2, 1989.

74. For the first reports on the creation of the Democratic Platform, see *New York Times* and *AP*, January 21 and 22, 1990. See also Julia Wishnevsky and Elizabeth Teague, "'Democratic Platform' Created in CPSU," *The Report on the USSR* 2, no. 5 (February 2, 1990): 7–9. See also *Pravda*, March 3, 1990, *Sovetskaya Belorussiya*, March 15, 1990, and *Literaturnaya gazeta*, no. 8 (1990): 2. For the Democratic Platform's views on the current situation of the CPSU, see Vladimir Lysenko, "Krizis partii i puti vykhoda iz nego," in the Estonian Communist Party Central Committee journal *Politika*, no. 1 (1990): 30–41.

75. *Gorizont*, no. 10 (1989).

76. Before the creation of the Democratic Platform was announced, Shostakovsky proposed reforms of the CPSU similar to those later advocated by the platform. See, for instance, Shostakovsky's article in *Sovetskaya kul'tura*, December 7, 1989.

77. For the text of the program of the Democratic Platform, see *Pravda*, March 3, 1990.

78. This suggestion was made by the secretary of the party organization at the Leningrad's Izhory factory, Yurii Arkhipov (*Pravda*, February 6, 1990). In his speech at the February plenum, Boris Yeltsin also expressed his support for the Democratic Platform (*Pravda*, February 6, 1990). In their turn, 750 representatives of Leningrad party organizations and clubs gathered on February 24–25 to pronounce their solidarity with the program of the Democratic Platform (*Sovetskaya molodezh'*, March 13, 1990).

79. *Pravda*, March 3, 1990.

80. The meeting of the Democratic Platform was reported by *TASS*, April 23, 1990. On April 19, *Reuters* said that Afanas'ev

left the CPSU. The expulsion of Chubais was revealed by *Reuters* on April 12. See also *Moscow News*, no. 16 (1990), which carried an article by Chubais, describing his expulsion.

81. Stankevich made his comment on RL Russian Service on April 24, 1990.

Chapter 7

1. Saulius Girnius, "Results of Lithuanian Supreme Soviet Elections," *Report on the USSR*, no. 10 (1990): 23–24.

2. One mass demonstration sponsored by the Interregional Group took place on February 4 (see *Izvestia*, February 6, 1990). Another took place on February 25 (*TASS, Central Television*, February 25, 1990).

3. *Izvestia*, March 1, 1990.

4. Ibid.

5. *Voprosy filosofii*, no. 8 (1987): 78–80; *Sovetskaya kul'tura*, October 7, 1989.

6. Julia Wishnevsky and Elizabeth Teague, "'Democratic Platform' Created in CPSU," *Report on the USSR*, no. 5 (1990): 7–9.

7. *Sovetskaya kul'tura*, March 17, 1990.

8. Ibid.

9. *Pravda*, February 8 and 9, 1990.

10. *Radio Moscow*, February 7, 1990.

11. *Pravda*, March 3, 1990.

12. *Izvestia*, February 27, 1990. See Dawn Mann, "An Argument for Legalizing Opposition to the CPSU," *Report on the USSR*, no. 11 (1990): 11–12.

13. As, for example, in the cases of the liberal democrats and the Christian democrats (*Central Television*, March 31 and April 8, 1990).

14. Klyamkin made this point several times in a contribution to the Radio Liberty Russian service.

15. See, for example, *Pravda*, March 28, 1990. For the text of the CPSU Central Committee statement, see *Pravda*, April 11, 1990.

16. *Pravda*, "Sel'skaya zhizn'," April 8, 1990.

17. See Dawn Mann, "Gorbachev Sworn in as President," *Report on the USSR*, no. 12 (1990): 1–4; Elizabeth Teague, "The

Powers of the Soviet Presidency," *Report on the USSR*, no. 12 (1990): 4–7.

18. Elizabeth Teague, "The Presidential Council Starts Its Work," *Report on the USSR* 2, no. 14 (1990): 1–3.

19. *TASS*, April 23, 1990.

20. Ibid., April 25, 1990.

Appendix

1. Unless otherwise stated, the information about sociopolitical movements is based on the article by Irina Snezhkova in *Obshchestvennye nauki*, no. 6 (1989): 110–23, and a survey of political groups in the USSR that appeared in *Novyi sobesednik*, no. 13 (1990).

2. See *Ogonek*, no. 8 (1990): 5.

3. The program of the Marxist Platform was published in *Moskovskaya pravda*, March 31, 1990, and *Pravda*, April 16, 1990. Although the Marxist Platform clearly intends to oppose the Democratic Platform, in an interview on Soviet television on April 14, 1990, its leaders condemned the CPSU Central Committee statement attacking the Democratic Platform.

4. *TASS*, April 1, 1990.

5. *Moscow News*, no. 13 (1990).

6. *Central Television*, March 31 and April 8, 1990; *Moscow News*, no. 17 (1990).

Index

Afanas'ev, Yurii, 25, 39, 73, 74, 77, 78, 79, 82
Afghan veterans groups, 50, 99
All-Union Association of Voters, 38
Anarcho-syndicalists, 40, 107n.29
Andreeva, Nina, 59, 61, 79
Anti-Semitism, 13, 71, 96
Armenian All-Nation Movement, 22
Autonomous republics, 23
Azerbaijan, 21

Baltic republics: Communist disunity and, 79; CPSU and, 20, 115n.72; elections and, 36–37, 43; independence movements, 85; "internationalist" movements and, 21, 95; Interregional Group and, 75; parliamentary groups, 97; popular fronts, 18–21, 53, 61; unofficial organizations in, 10–11; unofficial periodicals, 32. *See also specific countries, organizations*
Belorussia, 16, 21, 22, 37, 44–45, 48, 88, 112n.33
Belyaeva, Nina, 35
Burlatsky, Fedor, 2

Central Asian republics, 45
Chornovil, Vyacheslav, 44–5
Chubais, Igor, 79, 82
Civic Forum, 39
"Civil Action," 70, 96
Communist Party of the Soviet Union (CPSU): Baltic republics and, 20, 115n.72; decreasing prestige of, 8–9, 11, 48–49; Democratic Platform and, 25, 78–83, 87, 89–91, 96; disunity within, 79; informal candidates and, 42–43; opposition to, 86, 90; *perestroika* and, 81; response to informal groups, 53–54, 88–91; Soviet Constitution and, 3, 11, 76, 101n.5; unofficial media and, 34
Conferences, 26–29
Conservative groups, 65–68; elections and, 40–41, 43–44; internationalist movements and, 21, 95; *Pamyat'*, 13–15, 62, 96;